Rebel Wheels

PETER MOORE

From the library of
Danny Doyle
Raised on songs and stories

POOLBEG

First published 1990 by
Poolbeg Press
Knocksedan House
Swords Co Dublin

© Peter Moore 1990

ISBN 1 85371 069 5

Cover design by Steven Hope
Cover photograph taken at the time of the filming of
Bob Quinn's *Why Don't They Shoot People?*
Printed by the Guernsey Press
Vale Guernsey Channel Islands

I would like to dedicate this book to Liam's parents, Bill and Bridget Maguire

Acknowledgements

There are a few people and organisations I have to thank in relation to this book:

The late Paddy Byrne, with whom I first discussed the idea, for his encouragement and for making me realise that I would need quite a bit of financial assistance for the project. The initial finance came from the Irish Wheelchair Association, and I express my gratitude to the executive members.

Feidlim O'Reilly for his critical opinions and advice.

Aer Lingus for two complimentary tickets to New York. This visit enabled us to examine the movement of disabled people internationally, which was an important influence on Liam's thinking.

Liam's family, friends, and acquaintances for their willingness to grant me interviews.

Pat McCartan TD, who was most generous with his time when it came to explaining the legalities surrounding Liam's jury duty action and the Parkes Hotel case.

My mother for all the times she had to help me get ready early in the morning to go to interviews.

My sister Helen, Joe Leigh and Mrs Anne Colbert who alos helped on occasion.

Last but not least Brenda Kelly, my secretary thoughout the three years of research and writing without whose dedication the whole project would never have come to fruition.

Chapter 1

Liam Maguire was born on 3 September 1943. He was christened John William, but except among his Aer Lingus colleagues, he was commonly known as Liam. His parents, Bill and Bridget, both came from farming backgrounds in Longford. In 1936 Bill Maguire went to England because at that time of economic depression there were no jobs in Ireland for those who were not taking over the family farm. In 1938 when he was returning to England after a holiday he met Bridget on the boat. In 1941 they were married and settled in the south Dublin suburb of Dun Laoghaire.

According to Mrs Maguire, Liam quickly showed an active intelligence. He was educated by the Christian Brothers at Eblana Road, Dun Laoghaire. His brother Patrick remembers Liam as a very mature reader at a young age, reading writers such as Camus, Maupassant, Gogol. Eamonn Maguire, a schoolteacher himself, says his brother was terribly lazy in school: "Just didn't study—he got good grades without studying, but he never performed as well as he could have performed."

Yet Maguire would work hard at something that caught his interest. Patrick talks about Liam's hobbies of collecting birds' eggs, and stamp collecting. He was meticulous about these: birds' eggs were not just collected, they were brought home and every one had to be correctly labelled. He was particular about the type of stamps he collected, and they were all carefully catalogued. Later he took to building model aeroplanes, and again Patrick enthuses about Liam's patience in laying out the plans and the exacting way he cut the pieces to fit together. In later life he brought this precision to his many campaigns for disabled people.

Liam always stood out in a crowd. Donal Proctor, a friend from childhood into adult life, says Liam was used to being the centre of attention: "People paid attention to him." Proctor also remembers that he was a great dancer and good at the sort of sports he got involved in, although—except for basketball—he didn't take to team games. For most people it was his flow of comversation that made Liam pleasant company to be with. Donal Proctor and Patrick Maguire talk about Liam's having the best of clothes. When he was in the FCA he used wax when pressing his uniform to ensure a good crease in the trouser legs. Proctor says Liam read *The Tailor and Cutter* to keep up with changing fashons.

Talking about Liam in school, the boy-scouts and the FCA his brothers say he could accept authority as long as he had respect for his superior. Donal Proctor remembers being in serious trouble with one particular teacher in school when they were about sixteen years of age. Proctor was called from the classroom and was gone so long it was thought he was being expelled. Maguire was on the verge of organising a strike.

Surely here was the budding shop steward; the willingness to stand up for the underdog against an unjust establishment. But his brothers, and those who knew Liam then, are reluctant to see this as an incipient interest in left-wing politics. Donal Proctor says that as far as anyone is aware of adopting a political stance at nineteen, some of Liam's opinions would have been considered left-wing. "But," Proctor says, "I don't know any nineteen-year-old whose opinions would not be considered to be leftwing."

Liam's burning ambition was to be an airline pilot. At eighteen he was working in Ripple in Lancashire as a bus conducter. Bill Maguire saw in the newspaper that Aer Lingus had vacancies for trainee pilots. He sent the notice to Liam, who returned home. He passed the exams, but the medical showed that he had a slight heart condition. The heart was certain to right itself inside a year, and in the meantime Liam was to work as a clerk in the airport. He had only twelve months to wait to achieve his lifelong ambition. However, this wasn't to be. He had no way of knowing that fate would lead him in a completely different direction.

Chapter 2

It was 3.a.m. on Friday morning, 26 July 1962. A uniformed Garda knocked on Bill Maguire's door and told him that his eldest son, Liam, had had an accident. The Maguires' is a local authority house, of the type built by Dublin Corporation all over the city. Bill is a working man; before retiring he was a milkman with Premier Dairies.

That night Bill was on his own. His wife, Bridget, was in Longford nursing her sick mother and the younger children, Martin, Rory, Marion and Treasa, were with her. Bill went straight to St. Michael's Hospital, Dun Laoghaire where Liam lay unconscious. He went home and returned to St. Michael's hospital later that morning.

Life goes on, and from that second visit to the hospital Bill started out on his daily round. People for whom this morning was the same as any other wanted milk on the breakfast table.

Patrick Maguire heard about the accident when he woke up that Friday morning. He set out for the hospital and saw his father coming in the opposite direction. In Patrick's words: "We crossed paths. Dad stopped the truck. He had the window rolled down and he was crying. 'He's badly broken up, Patrick.' " Patrick continued to the hospital and found his brother in a bed near the ward door.

"My first impression when I walked around the door and saw him there was of somebody who was bruised around the face and bandaged around the forehead. But you couldn't see any damage other than that. The mouth I think was a bit bloody as well. He wanted a drink. I think he was given a drink, not by me. He was given a drink through a straw. That was the only way he could take it. He was obviously hallucinating at this stage," Patrick says, "because he started to ramble about ordering a bottle of beer and two straws, please."

Patrick started to cry, and a nun, "whom I could have cheerfully buried alive," demanded, "What's that boy doing in here crying. Get him out of here!"

Liam was moved to the Richmond Hospital in Dublin, and it was in the Richmond that they discovered he was paralysed. They could do nothing for him there. He was moved to the newly opened National Medical Rehabilitation Centre in Our Lady of Lourdes hospital in Dun Laoghaire, formerly a hospital for tuberculosis patients. According to Bill Maguire, Liam died and was revived three times during the journey from the Richmond Hospital to Rochestown Avenue.

On Sunday Bill travelled down to Longford to the home of Bridget's parents. He had come to take his wife home. Bridget couldn't understand why. It was not until they were in the car starting back that Bill told her of Liam's accident.

She could not believe it. She grabbed at Bill and began pulling his jacket open. "I don't know what came over me," she said. "I was just in a terrible state of shock."

"Is he at home?" she asked.

"No," replied Bill.

"Where is he?"

"They took him to Michael's Hospital and then to the Richmond."

"Oh God, his head," she thought.

"Now," her husband continued, "he's in the Lourdes."

He gave her very little detail until they pulled up at Our Lady of Lourdes Hospital. "Liam is in here. We'll go in to see him," he said simply.

When Bridget saw her first-born she says she did not recognise him. "The whites of his eyes were the colour of blood. His head was all bandaged and he was breathing heavily. One or two ribs were broken and had caused a lung to be punctured."

The sound of this heavy breathing accompanies the opening scene of Bob Quinn's film of Liam's rehabilitation. "When I first became conscious," Liam says in the film, "I don't think I was capable of thinking." He said he remembers a nurse with a name-tag on her uniform. "And I said 'Nurse Casby.' And she said 'How did you know my name?' 'By the tombstone on your chest,' because it seemed to me to be very big. But I might have been dreaming."

The doctors are doing their rounds. The staff nurse introduces the new patient.

"Good morning, Liam," says Dr Tom Gregg, Medical Officer of Our Lady of Lourdes Hospital. Dr Gregg turns to his assistant for the story of Liam's accident.

Liam was found lying beside his motorcycle and it seems his back had struck the kerb. The accident occurred on the Sandycove Road at the entrance to Bullock Harbour. After leaving his girlfriend home, Liam was going to collect his friend, Donal Proctor, in Dalkey. At that time the street lighting around Dalkey was switched off at midnight and Bill Maguire tells us that it was the sudden darkness that caused Liam to crash into the gatepost of Our

Lady's Manor nursing home.

The words the doctors use to describe Liam's injuries are detached and technical. It might be wrongly imagined that they are cold and indifferent. But this is their world. They are dealing with the same tragedies every day and they can't afford to show sympathy to you anymore than anyone else. Sympathy is no good to you now.

After a brief examination which confirms the loss of power and sensation below vertebra T7 just above the waist, the doctor again matter of factly says, "Good morning Liam" and goes.

Liam tells us he did not understand what they were talking about. "I didn't even for a moment consider the possibility that I was permanently disabled. I remember thinking to myself, 'OK, I'm going to walk out of here by Hallowe'en.' I crashed on 25 July."

Liam's idea of "walking out by Hallowe'en" comes up again and again when one talks to different people. Liam's friend Donal Proctor remembers Liam asking him to buy a new crash helmet. Later he talked about getting a car instead of a motorbike because with a car he would be out of the weather.

Nurse Brid Murphy was on holidays the day Liam was admitted. But she remembers a week or so later helping Mr Carey, the neurosurgeon from the Richmond Hospital, straighten a bone in his forehead which had been pushed in. Nurse Murphy told us this was the explanation for a small scar Liam had on his forehead. In later years this scar was barely noticeable except when Liam was making an impressive speech, when it seemed to add to the power and beauty of his words. It came down about half an inch from under his hairline, and was little more than a vertical wrinkle.

Back in the Maguire household Eamonn Maguire remembers that there was very little emotion shown during the daytime; but at night, when the children were in bed, Eamonn recalls hearing his father cry as he washed and shaved in the bathroom. Eamonn says this recurred for weeks after Liam's accident.

His father had bought the bike for Liam six or seven months before. The brothers are almost lost for words in their remembered enthusiasm for the new motorbike. Patrick recalls going for a ride on it with Liam. Rory helped his father to unload it from the van the day it came. It was a big bike, a 125cc. "It would have been the equivalent of driving a Harley Davidson today," says Rory.

For the first three weeks after the accident the family, especially Bill and Bridget, were going to the hospital any time they liked. Then they were told they could only come at visiting times. "It was the best news I had ever heard," says Mrs Maguire. Liam was out of danger.

Although any immediate danger had passed, Liam would be kept lying flat on his back for a further seven to nine weeks. "The treatment of a broken spine is basic to a fracture in any bone, which is to immobolise it," explains Dr Gregg. Thus, in Bob Quinn's film, we see that when Liam's bed was being made several of the nursing staff stood alongside the bed and all put their arms under him and raised him from the bed in a synchronised lift.

Brian Malone was in Our Lady of Lourdes Hospital alongside Liam. He had broken his neck in a swimming accident in his native Cork. Malone talked about his early period in hospital. He speaks about being "literally piped into hospital. Every bodily function, every item of every day is scheduled; you are awakened when they want you to waken, and you are allowed to go back to sleep when they want you to sleep. Fellows come and take bottles away. They come and put in food." As Malone talks he draws a picture of total dependence on others: "Like being in the womb again." Alternatively one thinks of scenes from a science fiction film, or a George Orwell novel.

The physiotherapist comes to exercise your legs. Your legs are paralysed, but they must be exercised to maintain the bloodflow. Without exercise the legs become calcified and would break with the least movement such as putting on a sock.

"Be very gentle with that leg," says Maguire. "It's the only right leg I've got."

The physiotherapist allows herself a chuckle while continuing her work.

"Yes," says physiotherapist Hilary Chatham. "It was all fast talk and witty answers with Liam. He kept up this brave front, but when working late I'd call to see him in the ward and I'd know Liam shed many a tear in the dark."

"There's always something special between spinal patients and their physios," says Mrs Chatham. "They spend so much time together. A very traumatic time for the patient and a caring—trying to instil hope—time for the physio." Liam calls it a love relationship, but perhaps it is closer to a maternal relationship tempered with a healthy objectivity not normal in a mother with her child; the relationship you have with a person who takes time teaching you a new skill or developing your talents, only this is much deeper and more fundamental.

The process of rehabilitation, a coming back—in Liam's case practically from the dead—continues.

One day, a physiotherapist asks would he like to sit up. "Tom," she calls, "could you give me a hand for a minute please?"

"Now, how does that feel?"

"Different," says Liam.

"I'm sure it does."

At this stage in Bob Quinn's film the camera angle shows us the ward as Liam sees it. He is still not allowed to sit completely upright. He can see the people moving about the ward, but he can't see the floor. We, the viewers, know that some of the people are in wheelchairs because they are low down and their heads and shoulders glide by the end of Liam's bed.

Liam says he does not remember when he first realised he was going to be paralysed. He says it must have come subconsciously from seeing others in wheelchairs.

Hilary Chatham remembers this. "Liam, being the intelligent person he was, knew in his heart, but did not want to face it."

"The slow raising to the vertical position again," as Liam puts it, continues, and the day draws near when you will be taken out of bed and put in a wheelchair.

"At this stage you are supposed to do occupational therapy. Make baskets and stuff like that. But I was interested in something that took a lot less effort," Liam says with a sense of humour. "I had played chess before I went into hospital. Became quite good at it in hospital. I won most of the time— some of the time?" His tone says: if you believe that you'd believe anything. However we are told he was good at the game and trade union colleagues have said he was like a chess-player during negotiations.

According to Hilary Chatham, being in the ward

is not too bad for the patient, but the first trip to the physiotherapy department is harrowing. "It's terrible to be in a wheelchair," she says, imagining herself in that position. "To see the world from a wheelchair for the first time. You can't feel your bottom even though you are sitting on it. And the physiotherapist is trying to teach you to balance on your own again."

"There was no time to be bored," says Brian Malone. "There was so much to be done, although none of it was terribly interesting. You could go in there and come out after two years without having to think for yourself. You'd go down to the OT (Occupational Therapy Department)—you'd go down to physio, you'd be called in for a case conference. Physically you'd think you could do all sorts of things, but you'd come up in the evenings and you'd be literally whacked. Then you might have a few visitors after tea."

Hilary Chatham tells us that when you visit the physiotherapy department for the first time you are treated like a baby. You are put on a couch and splints are put on your legs—you have no feelings in the lower half of your body. The physiotherapist then stands you in front of a full-length mirror and pushes you from side to side.

You are begining the process of learning to balance.

We see Liam tentatively pushing his wheelchair into the physiotherapy department or "gym," as he calls it. Maybe his general approach and express-ions do, as Brian Malone says, suggest contempt, but there is also the hesitancy of entering a strange place where you know something is expected of you but you are not sure what.

Liam talks about seeing people "pulling weights,

standing by parallel bars and so on. And you say to yourself—God, have I got to do that?" Again the impish, slightly self-mocking sense of humour.

"Ready for work?" asks the physiotherapist.

"No!" Which means a reluctant "yes."

"Push," says the physiotherapist as she helps him transfer from the wheelchair on to the couch.

"You're doing all this on your own, y'know." Maguire continues the wititicisms.

"Push again. Come on. Well done."

Liam progresses from sitting on the couch in front of the mirror, holding on for dear life as the physiotherapist pushes him backwards, forwards, and from side to side—standing in front of the mirror—walking between parallel bars with calipers on his legs—walking with crutches, still with calipers. He will never be able to walk except for exercise purposes. After ten steps he tells us he's "absolutely panned," shaking with exhaustion on the two crutches.

Liam is pulling weights. He still does not accept that he is going to be in a wheelchair. When some other patient pulls eighteen pounds he is determined to pull twenty pounds. It is all a determined effort towards walking out of hospital. But Hallowe'en is drawing nearer.

Occupational therapy is a very important part of a paraplegic's rehabilitation. The aim is to give something constructive to do so that the person will not be in a vacuum.

When Liam Maguire first went to OT they asked him would he make baskets.

"No—no—no—no!"

"Make carpets?"

"Nope."

"Well, what will you do? You'll have to do

something."

Liam had been building model aeroplanes since the age of nine. So he tells us that for his occupational therapy he built a First World War fighter, an Albatross D5.

Still the dream of walking out! He wrongly believed that if he stayed in hospital long enough and with all the medical attention and therapy he would eventually be able to walk. He did not want to go home because he was afraid.

"I was used to being with people in wheelchairs; people who knew the way I felt."

As Brian Malone puts it: "with the activity and business of the hospital, there was a great sense of progress and a feeling that progress was unlimited. But the big disappointment would come when you'd go home. It's all very well going out to this party or on that night out from the hospital. But then you realise the world is not like a hospital; it isn't all progress and it isn't all on the level and people don't understand." Malone goes on to express how you are no longer a normal person just sitting in the pub having a pint. You are now an object of morbid curiosity. People are amazed that you are there doing a normal everyday thing such as having a pint.

Liam was being discharged. We can only guess at what he was feeling. There must have been a mixture of anticipation and fear. "Of course he had been particularly fortunate both with regard to his family and to his work," Dr Gregg says in the Bob Quinn film. We hear that Dr Dempsey of Aer Lingus had visited him while in hospital and assured him they would employ him in his former capacity of traffic clerk.

The different hues in Liam's character came out

as we talked to people who knew him in hospital. They talk of him being arrogant and self-centred. "I would say there was absolutely no suggestion of any social awareness or involvement, or selflessness, about Liam at that stage," says Brian Malone.

Noel O'Toole, who was paralysed from a gun-shot wound received while serving with the Irish army in the Congo, says: "He was two different people at the time he was in hospital compared with the time he had left the hospital and was out on his own. He was much quieter when he was here." We spoke to O'Toole in Our Lady of Lourdes Hospital where he works as a receptionist and telephonist. The two staff nurses, Sr Marie and Nurse Brid Murphy, were with us. O'Toole agrees with Sister Marie that Liam was very aggressive later on.

At the same time they agree that Liam had a kind heart. There are numerous stories of him being generous to others when he himself was fully rehabilitated and out and about.

He told Hilary Chatham when there were young people in the hospital that he would bring in and play records of the past year for them, because music was the first thing that got to him after leaving the hospital. "The last time you heard that tune you were at such a party or dancing with someone." He wanted to get that out of their systems before they left hospital.

Nurse Murphy told a story of a girl from Clare who had family upsets at the same time as her accident. He used to take this girl out of the hospital and bring her back later than he should have.

He had no patience with what he saw as unnecessary rules and regulations, and felt that having to be in the hospital at a set time was contrary to the principles of rehabilitation. When a doctor told him he couldn't look at his X-Rays, Liam answered, "It's my body."

These are possibly the first indications of his fierce belief in the right of disabled people to control their own lives.

Chapter 3

Home again—home sweet home—there's no place like home. But for Liam Maguire at the age of twenty, being discharged from hospital was the enforcement of the bitter truth. In one radio interview Liam talked about the period between coming home from hospital and returning to work in Aer Lingus: "I was very much alone and introverted. I spent a lot of the time in, I suppose, melancholy. I did the obvious things like going out to parties mainly because I was forced to by various mates of mine, my brothers and that." He continued humorously: "It's very hard to resist a couple of six footers who grab hold of your wheelchair and start pushing. But a lot of the time I spent in my room literally looking out at the real world on the street, or playing records and being nostalgic and tearful until I was more fully occupied in the situation of doing a normal day's work."

In 1968 he wrote, "The only way to know life in a wheelchair is to experience it. Marlon Brando did this when he acted in Kubrick's film *The Men*. Most people have neither the time nor the inclination to spend a long time in a wheelchair, they don't need to, understandably so. What I do not understand are the inflexible misconceptions in our society about people confined to wheelchairs: how can one have an accurate knowledge of something he has never experienced? It is a preposterous presumption on the part of the individual who is not disabled to say, or to think 'I know how you feel.' Liam said he wanted to get people to admit "I don't know how you feel, I don't know anything about your views on life," then to seek to find the truth through a genuine interest stemming from a human motive.

Dr Jerry Dempsey, then general manager of Aer Lingus, recalls visiting Liam in his home. Dr Dempsey explains that it was customary for him to be given a list from the personnel department of staff members who were on sick leave for more than three months. "His name was on the list that I got just prior to Christmas 1962. I went to the rehabilitation hospital on Rochestown Avenue and they told me he was out on parole for the weekend; he was making progress and doing well so they let him go home." Dr Dempsey explains that he did not know where Liam lived, but got the address at the hospital. "I eventually reached his home and he had a friend in with him in his house—not a very big house—and I could see very quickly, because of the noise, it was just full of children."

Dr Dempsey continues his narrative: "I asked him about himself and what the doctors thought about his progress. 'Do you think you will be able to work again?' I didn't at this particular time say anything to him about returning to work. I merely asked him the general question: did he think, or did the doctors think, that he would be able to do work of some kind."

Liam's mother says there was talk of him being employed in Aer Lingus's booking offices in Dun Laoghaire, but Liam wanted to get back to the airport. Aeroplanes were his first love and if he could not be a pilot, then he wanted to be as near as possible to them and to have the sound of them in his ears.

Dr Dempsey tells us he then had to report back on the people he visited and how they were progressing. "I particularly referred to this young man, a man of high spirits. I realised that the accident must have had a great effect on him. I didn't know him before and I wasn't able to make a real comparison. But the fact that he was such a high-spirited person certainly suggested to me that he wasn't going to lie down under his accident."

Accepting your disability and lying down under it are two very different, if not opposite, concepts. Liam says it was two years after the accident before he fully accepted the fact of being disabled. In the documentary film *Why Don't They Shoot People?* produced by Bob Quinn for RTE television, Liam said, "A job is absolutely the most important thing. When you are leaving hospital, if you haven't got some sort of positive occupation, something which has a monetary reward—that you are working and capable of supporting yourself—this is absolutely the most important thing. I knew that I was going back to a very good job." He then gave full credit to Aer Lingus for affording him the opportunity and continued, "I think my whole attitude, my whole point of view, would have changed if I didn't have a job to go back to."

His brothers remember the time prior to Liam going back to work. Patrick says that because he was in college for most of the time, he was removed from Liam during the most difficult period. "I only saw him on visits and I know on these occasions the problem—the difficulty—of moving outside again. Round about that stage we had a conversation..."— Patrick paused mid-sentence to emphasise his absolute certainty—"round about then he told me that whatever he took up he was going to work very hard at and he reckoned he would burn himself out by forty." Patrick is certain, however, that this was in no sense a death-wish.

"He spent a long time after he came home from hospital just sitting in his room staring out the window," says Eamonn.

Talking about the period immediately after Liam left hospital, Donal Proctor says, "To a degree he had become institutionalised. From my re-collection—it's not something I think about much—they had to work on him to get him out of the hospital to go home." Donal Proctor stresses that Liam was coming out from hospital into a locale where he had always been centre stage. He was coming out, at that time, in every sense a broken man.

In September 1963 Liam got a car with hand controls and went back to work. This was a major step on the road back. As we will see from his mother's account, there was no sudden complete change. Yet there is no under-estimating the importance of employment to a disabled person. If the occupation provides an income comparable with that of his able-bodied peers it gives the individual self-confidence among his family and friends. This would have been important to Liam, and work had the additional social benefit of mixing with colleagues.

Unlike most accident victims, Liam had no compensation coming to him. The finance for his first car came from a variety of sources, mainly from his airport colleagues raising funds by raffles and dances. Liam said he also borrowed money from the credit union at the airport.

"He went to work in the car and that was alright," says Mrs. Maguire, "but I don't think he accepted that he would be in the wheelchair for the rest of his life."

His mother says people would stop, stand, and watch him getting in or out of his car. In the early sixties there were few disabled people moving about in society and those who came outdoors had to endure being treated as a curiosity. The extent of this is much less now than twenty-five years ago as people have become relatively used to seeing disabled people in public places.

Patrick Maguire speaks of the "dread" he had of Liam moving outside the house. "I can remember in the early stages going through a phase of thinking, 'Oh Jesus, don't go out —please don't go out.'" Or "When we go out to the cinema, theatre airport, hotel, please let there be wheelchair access so that there won't be another row." With these words Patrick evokes the terrible fear of embarrassment he felt for his brother. He wanted Liam to lead a normal life, but society would not allow this. Patrick continues, "As I said; it was pioneering ground. It was very difficult for me to cope with, and I thought 'Jeez, what must it be like for this guy having to cope with this?'" Patrick points out that as well as people's attitudes there were the added problems of accessibility. "You want to get into a cinema and you can't. You've got a revolving door, you've got steps, and you've got all this hassle." Patrick reiterates being very conscious: "If this is very alien for me—out with a guy in a wheelchair— what's it like for the guy who's sitting there. And that's where he was marvellously courageous, because at that stage he said 'Fuck it, here I come, no way am I going to back into a corner.'"

"That's what made Liam as he became, I think," Martin takes up his brother's point. "The only identity that he could be allowed by the world at large was as a disabled man in a wheelchair. That's the only thing he could possibly be, and that's the thing he wouldn't allow to be imposed on him. There were a lot of other ways he saw himself and that was the least."

The brothers, particularly Eamonn, felt Liam gradually got more and more confident when he went back to Aer Lingus and established himself there.

Martin Dully, formerly sales manager of Aer Lingus, remembers Liam as being part of the traffic team. "That was really the elite of the company." The traffic team dealt with passengers, pilots and hostesses. "They did—what was very important in those days—weight and balance sheets which meant the centre of gravity of the aircraft was where it should be when the plane took off."

We spoke to a number of Liam's colleagues in what seemed like a rest-room-cum-canteen-cum-cloakroom. We tried to imagine Liam in their midst; sometimes quiet, but at other times dominating the company as was usual in his social life. "If he was here now," says John McCarthy, "You'd probably hear an unmerciful bang and that would be Maguire having taken the side off his wheelchair to give the wall (made of wood) a wallop." This would not be a call for help—Maguire was fiercely independent—more a larger-than-life character announcing his own arrival.

"I think his character developed after his accident," Eamonn Teeling says. "Whatever was there before seems to have been drowned out by the character in the wheelchair." This appears to be true, as none of the airport people contactable had any clear memories of Liam *out* of the wheelchair.

Barry Cullen explained the nature of Liam's job. He was responsible for the general co-ordination of all materials and passengers going on the aircraft and the overall weight and balance. He would communicate with the flight crew and ensure that everything was completed on time.

In Bob Quinn's film we see Liam at a desk upon which there are papers and with a microphone in front of him. A voice comes from an intercom "Echo Kilo D 867 from London estimating ground at four zero, one three zero passengers and three thousand deadload. The figures for return if you're ready to copy." Liam responds, "go ahead Echo Kilo. I understand you're estimating at four zero with one three zero passengers and three thousand kilos deadload. Will you go ahead with your return figures please?"

His colleagues say he was very thorough on the job. "He would have his head down on the desk and you wouldn't think he was with you, but when something was said he would come alive and you knew he was on top of everything."

His airport colleagues are just some of the people who talk about Liam's driving. Many say he was not only fast, but downright reckless. They say it was because of his disability. It was a way of working off his frustrations and he didn't care what happened. However, Terry Davis, a colleague from air traffic and seemingly a close friend says, "Liam lived life in the fast lane. Everything he did was at speed and driving was no different."

One long weekend a number of staff members decided to go to Shannon. Most of the party took a plane, but Maguire decided to take his car, so he could be independent, and go where he liked once he got there. Terry Davis and Barry Cullen said they would go with him. Their journey started at McDaid's, a famous literary pub in Dublin, with stops at other pubs en route. On the Limerick Road they caught up with a Morris Minor indicating to turn right. When Liam went to pass on the inside the Morris unexpectedly turned left. Maguire drives up on the bank. The two lads sit tight, frightened for their lives, while Maguire is muttering ferociously. Eventually he swerves down off the bank, saying something about it being like Vietnam.

Donal Proctor also gallops into a boisterous monologue at the mention of Liam's first car. "The Ford Anglia," he exclaims, as if remembering an unfortunate mule which had been cruelly brutalised throughout its life. He talks about Liam having banged that car up a lot and each time repairing the damage with fillers. "There must have been half a stone of fillers in that car."

Proctor talks about driving to places like Bray and Greystones. Sometimes it was with Liam, himself and their two girlfriends, sometimes it was just Liam and Donal and other times they would have a friend with them. He talks about bringing flasks of coffee and Bovril sandwiches on these trips. He recalls several accidents Liam had when he was with him; driving into ditches and shouting at his passenger for not pulling the handbrake after Proctor had climbed into the back seat for fear of his life. Once Liam drove against the traffic on a one-way street and then fired verbal abuse at the driver of the car he crashed into for driving on the wrong side of the road. The other driver could only utter a series of "buts" against Maguire's verbal assault. "I don't think he accepted that it was a one way street," says Proctor.

"Sunday morning was the usual thing," Proctor says. "I'd call down to his place, and we might go up to Vico Road, and Liam used to do the Ximines crossword in the *Sunday Times*. We'd go there and we'd pretend to do the Ximines crossword. He'd get about eighty percent of it and we'd get about three or four words."

At one time Liam got his car painted red. The memory of this leads Proctor to talk about Ken Murphy, whom he describes as a very old friend of Liam's and a man with a quick wit. Donal says he met Ken at mass one Sunday morning. They were walking home past Liam's house, and the car was outside. "Did you see yer man's car?" says Proctor. Murphy replies sombrely: "Drives the thing like a fire engine, might as well look like a fire engine."

Donal Proctor's words show one side of Liam's character. A young man, some might say immature, but it's normal for a man in his early twenties to indulge in fast driving and Liam possibly wanted to prove to his friends that he was no less macho than they were.

But Liam was hurting. Hilary Chatham, who had been his physiotherapist in hospital, and was just married at the time, writes of Liam coming to see her and helping her make her first Christmas cakes. "I think he came to sound me out on various things he wanted to do." She evokes a childlike image of Liam, still feeling hurt and unsure of himself. "My view was always that you can do anything you want to do, if not one way then another."

There was a soft and gentle side to Liam. His brothers Martin and Patrick say family life was important to him. To people who didn't know him intimately, this was not always apparent because he was so independent. Patrick says he compartmentalised his life and determined that the brothers and sisters were to carry no burden because he was in a wheelchair.

"Just Saturdays," Eamonn takes over from Patrick, "when he wanted a bath."

"Nobody goes out on Saturdays until I've had my bath," Rory recalls Liam's standpoint. This was before he got a government grant to build a bathroom on the ground floor for his own use. It took two or three of the brothers to carry him upstairs in the wheelchair. Patrick says there was no way Liam was going to be carried in anybody's arms. "He went up those stairs in the wheelchair and he came back down the stairs in the wheelchair."

The stairs in the Maguire house are barely wide enough for the wheelchair and Rory recalls scratching his knuckles against the wall. One can almost see the condescending smirk on Liam's face as he playfully teased his youngest brother saying "Aren't you the fucking eejit."

The depth of feeling Liam had for his family comes through when one is talking to his sisters, Marion and Theresa, of whom he was very possessive. The youngest of the family, Theresa, was five when Liam had his accident, and Marion was eight. They laugh about Liam giving stern warnings to both their boyfriends as they were about to get married, saying they could always "win Daddy over," but they needed Liam's approval first.

Talking about Liam's leadership qualities—he was the wheelchair general, the brains, while ablebodied people were his brawn—Patrick Maguire wonders whether, if the accident had not occurred and Liam had become a pilot, he would have been happy to settle into comfortable middle class "oblivion."

Eamonn Maguire thinks that Liam's time with Bob Quinn, making the documentary film of his medical rehabilitation and taking it to Berlin in 1965, was the awakening of his political awareness. Around the same time there were two other things in Liam's life that indicate the road he was to travel. In 1965 Liam was first elected shop steward by his colleagues in Dublin Airport, and the same year he began lobbying David Andrews TD. in an effort to have the government lessen the financial burden of motoring for disabled drivers.

Bob Quinn had arranged to meet Liam at Searson's pub in Baggot Street. Quinn was there first, sitting pensively with his drink in front of him, expecting to see somebody who needed help all the time. Suddenly the pub doors explode inwards. Bob Quinn describes "this fellow" in a wheelchair going the length of the pub extremely fast and coming to a sudden stop. "How're ya, sport," says Maguire. Bob Quinn says he was taken aback, but then he sat down and they got drunk together.

At closing time Liam said "C'mon, there's a party out in Malahide."

"Malahide," says Quinn, "but that is...'

"Ah c'mon out o' that! Are you a man or a mouse!"

Bob Quinn says: "So he drove me out to Malahide and frightened the shit out of me with his driving."

Quinn says his impression of Liam that first night at the party is that he was always trying to show that he was absolutely normal, "just like one of us." And in fact at one stage he became aggressive—mock aggressive—and he took the arm off his wheelchair and threatened to cut a fellow's head off.

"Although," says Bob, "it was quite humorous.'

Bob Quinn says that when he first met Liam, Liam was "hell bent" on becoming a millionaire. Donal Proctor also said that Liam was a budding entrepreneur and wanted to make a million quick. "He was a normal fella," Proctor insists. "He aspired to having cars, money, women and houses. That's what he wanted…just like us all."

At the same time Quinn saw that the seeds of the future socialism were there in the form of Liam's intelligence and his insight through his disability into the fundamentals of socialism. "At that time I think he was saying 'the world is as it is—it's a jungle—and it's every man for himself.' But when thinking about his particular position he was saying, 'If every man is for himself then where does that leave me, because I am not entirely independent?' " He was, as we have been told by Nurse Brid Murphy and physiotherapist Hilary Chatham, concerned about disabled people whom he would visit in Our Lady of Lourdes hospital and try to help through the anguish he had been through himself. It is a natural progression for a disabled person with intelligence to realise that hardship is not only connected with disability.

Thus we can assume that Liam progressed from thinking about the difficulties of his fellow disabled people to realising the degradation of grinding poverty and the demands of other minorities to have full human rights. In Bob Quinn's words, he didn't have a conversion like St Paul on the road to Damascus.

Bob Quinn talks about himself being very left-wing and anti-establishment at that time. "Indeed I used to have great arguments with Liam about his ambition to be a millionaire and a great capitalist and I used to say, 'When you become a capitalist, I'm going to shoot you, you bastard.' "

However, if Bob Quinn did start Liam on the socialist road, they came to a fork—although the prongs were not very wide apart—and they both took different directions.

When Bob Quinn made the film on Liam's rehabilitation he was employed by RTE. These were turbulent years for the newly-opened television station. Programme-makers such as Quinn were in open conflict with administrative management, and an account of these years (the book *Sit Down and be Counted*) was published in 1969. In it we learn that Bob Quinn finally left RTE because upon returning after a year in America he found the station "had all the verbal trappings of a factory..." Quinn's artistic temperament could not accept the discipline of a big organisation whereas Maguire was very much at home in the corporate world. Perhaps Quinn's move to Connemara in the west of Ireland was a final opting out on his part, whereas Maguire was almost in love with the industrialised city. We have been told when Maguire saw a field of green grass, his instinct was to say it was a good site for a factory.

Bob Quinn says he did grow away from Liam in the latter's activist years. "I came to a point,' says Quinn, "when I was living away from the Pale and it seems to me he was getting involved in a Pale dominated—or Dublin dominated—perspective on society. The thing I would have eventually dis-agreed with Liam about was the extreme of his anti-rural or pro-Dublin bias."

Liam immersed himself in the intellectual life of Dublin. Novelist/playwright Lee Dunne writes of first meeting Liam in The Bailey, which he describes as a literary pub then owned by John Ryan, himself a writer and a well-known painter. "That day," continues Lee Dunne, "we were both intent on getting drunk and the crack was great when this actor asked Liam if he was ever going to be alright. I answered the question in what might well be described as a forceful manner: 'Can't you see he's alright now?' which made Maguire laugh. The bould Liam didn't need any help to hold his corner and everybody else's." Indeed, from other people's descriptions, it seems that Liam was seldom so passive when anyone treated him with pity in such a way.

Folk singer Ronnie Drew of the Dubliners, writer Ulick O'Connor, and various politicians talk of meeting Liam in Groome's Hotel which was opposite the Gate Theatre in Cavendish Row. Groome's Hotel in the 1960s and early '70s was frequented by people from artistic and political life till the early hours. Ronnie Drew says, "He wasn't treated as a person in a wheelchair—it wasn't noticed because he managed his wheelchair so well. He could get in and out of anywhere."

Liam was also a regular in O'Donoghue's pub in Merrion Row, a meeting place mostly for traditional musicians. Physiotherapist Hilary Chatham writes of seeing less and less of Liam. "Now when he achieved something he would phone to tell me. I was invited to O'Donoghue's pub one Saturday to meet his friends, Lee Dunne and the Dubliners. I was supposed to be impressed and I was, but he got very cheeky so I whispered to him if he didn't behave I'd clip his ear in front of everyone." So Liam achieved the goal of rehabilitation. He was living a full life in society—it was natural that he'd be flattered at being accepted in the company of writers and intellectuals—but he was never going to be too important for Hilary Chatham to give him a "clip on the ear." As she says herself, "I was probably more like a sister or a mother at this stage."

If Bob Quinn started Liam on his socialist journey, Oliver Donoghue was one of those who trod alongside him every step of the way. Donoghue writes, "My first contact with Liam was as a researcher on a series of 'Youth' discussion programmes being presented on RTE television by Bunny Carr. After the making of Bob Quinn's film, Liam frequented Madigan's pub in Donnybrook, and was well known to many people in RTE. "

Oliver Donoghue: "Liam's appearances on television and his outspoken criticisms of the hypocrisies of Irish society, his demand for rights for disabled people (instead of charity) and so on made a huge impact on the Ireland in the middle to late sixties—an Ireland which was still extremely conservative and saw the disabled as people to be pitied and helped."

At the close of Bob Quinn's film Liam says he is quite content to be in a wheelchair, that he didn't particularly want to be able to run or dance. Many people don't believe this. They say he never accepted being in a wheelchair. On the other hand Maria Cassidy, who became closest to him, says she wouldn't have done so if Liam indulged himself in self-pity. What he did not accept—and he would never compromise—was being treated differently because of his handicap.

Chapter 4

While Liam was in hospital and convalescing at home, an organisation in which he was destined to have a leading role was in its infancy. In November 1960, eighteen months before Liam's accident, nine disabled people met in the Round Room of the Mater Hospital in Dublin, and founded the Irish Wheelchair Association.

The dynamic force behind the newly formed IWA was Fr Leo Close. Fr Paddy Lewis, disabled with polio and then studying for the priesthood, was also in the Round Room. Lewis sees Jack Kerrigan and Oliver Murphy, motivated by Leo Close, as "the trinity that began it."

Jack Kerrigan and Oliver Murphy spoke to us about the situation which led to the first official meeting. Jack Kerrigan had been disabled for ten years, and in the mid 1950s, Fr Leo Close became confined to a wheelchair. Oliver Murphy had had his accident in 1959. Murphy and Kerrigan spoke about Leo Close as a pleasant companion but one who had a dynamo inside which wouldn't let him rest. "Day and night," says Kerrigan, "he was always pushing, pushing, pushing." Oliver Murphy humorously remembers the wheelchair priest as a fidget; a man too preoccupied with the business in hand to be concerned with something as insignificant as his own cigarettes and lighter which he would throw onto the person beside him. "You had to get to know him," Murphy says, "or you would end up carrying a load of stuff that wasn't yours."

By 1960 the tuberculosis endemic to Ireland had been cleared away and, according to Oliver Murphy, the RTB (Rehabilitation Tuberculosis, which later became the Rehabilitation Institute) were searching for new areas where they felt their help was needed. They started to think about the physically disabled.

The first venture for RTB was to take a small team to the paraplegic Olympics in Rome. Five of the nine who were destined to be in the Round Room the following November made up that team. Jack Kerrigan was a swimmer; Oliver Murphy was an archer; Fr Leo Close played table-tennis and was an archer; Joan Horan was a swimmer and archer and Jimmy Levins's abilities lay in field events.

Oliver Murphy and Jack Kerrigan tell us that the five in Rome could see from the RTB's handling of them that they hadn't the right attitude to take charge of the affairs of disabled people. Murphy and Kerrigan are emphatic that they were not badly treated while in Rome. "But," continues Jack Kerrigan, "we were regarded as having no minds, and no thoughts of our own. We would be told where to be and what to do."

"Cripples and imbeciles?" my assistant suggested.

"Absolutely!" Kerrigan responds.

"We spoke to an awful lot of people at that games," says Oliver Murphy, "about how things were going in their countries, particularly Dutch and Americans. We formed the opinion, Fr Leo more than anyone else, that this was the time that at home in Ireland something should be started specifically to help people in wheelchairs."

Remembering their thoughts on forming the new organisation, Jack Kerrigan says that it wasn't so important that the disabled had complete control, "but that their views would be in there at the very top."

Kerrigan says that both Close and himself had had experience of being helped by organisations for the disabled at the time. "I had had the RTB to my house," says Kerrigan, "and they were going to help me," Kerrigan's voice lowers to a bitter cynicism, "by getting me to sell pools—tickets round my friends—and I would get twenty-five percent and they would get seventy-five, and that's how they were going to help me."

Kerrigan says Fr Leo Close had first mentioned starting a new organisation in August 1958 when they first met. There were plenty of charities at that time, but according to Jack Kerrigan none of them had any positive outlook for people in wheelchairs. "They all had the same idea, that if you were in a wheelchair you were past it. That was just a degree too far," he says emphatically. "And the nine people there were not of that opinion. We knew we weren't past it."

When the five came back from Rome in September 1960, Fr Leo Close, the only one with a car at that time, commuted between Dublin and Drogheda where Oliver Murphy and Jack Kerrigan lived. Meetings took place in the house of Kerrigan who, according to Fr Paddy Lewis, was very useful in fund-raising and was later to become chief executive officer of the Association for a time. Advertisements were placed in the national papers in an effort to contact other disabled people.

Once the Association had been formally established, with a board of management which, according the Fr Paddy Lewis, had to have a number of disabled people, the next important step was the setting up of quarterly socials. When one is interested in the political history, there might be a tendency to dismiss the social side as just tea and biscuits. But according to Oliver Murphy, the socials were, and still are, a cornerstone of the Association. "It helps keep committees together, and keeps people working towards something that is positive." Indeed it was through going to weekly socials in Fairview, Dublin that the present author first came in contact with the IWA.

Although Paddy Lewis was in the Round Room he was studying for the priesthood and didn't have a car at the time. He says he didn't really get involved in the Association until the end of 1961 or '62. He was then working towards a social science degree, which he felt would complement his efforts in the IWA.

From our research it appears the development of the IWA was very much tied in with the newly established National Medical Rehabilitation Centre in the former TB hospital on Rochestown Avenue, Dun Laoghaire. According to Jack Kerrigan, its medical director, Dr Tom Gregg, had a very positive view of the physically disabled. Oliver Murphy and Jack Kerrigan recall organising the IWA pools from the hospital and moving from one ward to the next as the conversion from a TB hospital to a spinal unit was taking place. Being anxious to help and because their involvement lent prestige to the new organisation, Dr Gregg and his assistant, Dr Colm Wilmot, joined the IWA board.

However, Fr Paddy Lewis says he had a feeling that Doctor Gregg saw the Association merely as an adjunct to the hospital. From the early years until the late 1960s the main issue and source of controversy in the IWA was the building of a hostel. According to Oliver Murphy, the hostel was to be a place for people to live in Dublin while they were trained for employment. Lewis says that he thought Dr Gregg was using the hostel and the IWA as a way of achieving something he needed: such as freeing some hospital beds he needed for other people.

It would be unreasonable to criticize a doctor harshly for taking the doctor's point of view. Medical treatment is the most important need of a person immediately upon suffering serious physical injury, and to want to provide this as efficiently as possible is the trained instinct of the medical profession. It is equally important that when everything medically has been done the disabled individual is enabled to get back into society and to live as normal a life as possible. It is for the latter purpose, and to change the public view of those with physical handicaps, that the IWA was formed.

Fr Lewis says he was never happy with the idea of the hostel because it meant spending a great deal of money on something that would benefit only a very limited number of people. He also began to get indications that a certain number of members were unhappy with the idea of a hostel.

Oliver Murphy says the crunch came at a well-attended meeting in the IWA offices at Pearse Street in Dublin. Murphy and Kerrigan say that the meeting was packed with people who were not part of the IWA who were there in order to carry the argument in support of a hostel. However the doctors failed in their bid and those who were against the hostel and wanted more social services won the day. Perhaps this night is equal in significance to the night in the Round Room when the Association was founded. If the discussion had gone the other way, it is likely the IWA would have developed like all the other organisations dominated by the orthopaedic professionals, with disabled people having only a token presence at the centre of power.

The controversy continued and the hostel idea was not yet quite dead. In 1967 it was decided that the Association would do a survey of the members' needs. Again some of the board took the autocratic view that they knew what these needs were. Others felt that the members should speak for themselves. Fr Lewis says he had the training to do the survey, but felt that if he did it could be suspected the survey was biased. The survey was carried out by a graduate from University College Dublin, and it concluded that a hostel was not a priority in what the members wanted from the Association.

It seems this was the end of the hostel, and the doctors' efforts to have the IWA attached to the National Medical Rehabilitation Centre. One of the first functions of the newly appointed IWA chief executive officer, Phil O'Meachair, was to tell Jack Kerrigan to write a one thousand pound cheque for the architect, and ask him to go away.

The IWA did provide funds to build the Fr Leo Close Sports Hall at the Dun Laoghaire hospital. Fr Lewis remembers himself and other members being annoyed over this. "We were being used, period, that's it," says Lewis, anger still perceptible in his voice after twenty years. But Jack Kerrigan says the Fr Leo Close Hall had been promised and was built as a return for the help of Mother Bernadette in very early months when the Association organised their fund-raising campaign from the hospital wards.

During these years, Liam Maguire was very much on the fringe of the IWA and it must be said he was not very popular with the founders who were then running the Association. There is also a strong suggestion of Liam being arrogant. Jack Kerrigan particularly says that he asked Liam to join the Association on numerous occasions only to be told, "My social life is too great, Jack, I'm too busy." They use words like "smart alec" to describe him, and Fr Lewis agrees he was "a bit of a maverick."

One suspects that Liam had no patience with taking over an organisation and proving that disabled people could merely do things—such as fund raising—as efficiently as able-bodied professionals. It has been said that he was frustrated with the IWA being, as he saw it, only concerned with its own bank balance, and Jack Kerrigan has admitted, "We were building up funds without any clear objective of what to use them for."

Already Liam was bringing the issue of disability onto a wider battlefront. From 1965 he was lobbying politicians—notably David Andrews TD—to have disabled drivers exempted from road tax. His father told us he was writing to European countries and finding out more about facilities for people in wheelchairs. Liam has said he resigned from the IWA board to begin the car-tax campaign. Jack Kerrigan said that at one meeting Liam smashed the table with the arm of his wheelchair.

There is also the factor of Liam's relative youth. He was still in his early twenties, and, as Phil O'Meachair puts it: "He was an aggressive tough young man who was finding it hard to come to terms with all this energy, and vitality, and everything that was in him that was going to have to exist in a wheelchair."

Phil O'Meachair, the Irish Wheelchair Association's chief executive officer from 1967, recalls his first meeting with Liam. "Having seen RTE's film and read of his campaign for motor tax remission for physically handicapped drivers, and occasionally heard none-too-complimentary comments about him, I was anxious to meet *l'enfant terrible* of the wheelchair fraternity," O'Meachair wrote in *Push*, the Association's journal.

Because of their close similarities and the vast differences between them a reflection on Phil O'Meachair's character make-up is one way to get an insight into Liam Maguire. Like Maguire had, O'Meachair has a fine command of written and spoken language. Liam could fill a room with his voice as an actor fills a theatre. Entering conversation with Phil O'Meachair is like going on a calm lake in a small boat, but you never know when a storm is going to blow, only to subside just as quickly to a relative calm. Both were aggressive, but this aggression is an expression of their commitment. Liam saw himself as a city man through and through—a child of the cosmopolitan metropolis. The writer remembers O'Meachair proudly introducing himself as a "country boy" to a large gathering of IWA members. Liam professed himself a socialist, whereas Phil is an admirer of the entrepreneurial spirit.

Talking of Liam as a newcomer, O'Meachair says "the founders were all relatively privileged; they'd all had a good education, they'd all suffered disability due to accidents."

The IWA founder members were of rural background, whereas Liam grew up in the stark white concrete of working-class Sallynoggin.

O'Meachair evokes the name of the English playwright, John Osborne, and proclaims that Liam was "one of the angry young men." There are those who say that Liam was angry for himself, feeling hurt and loss of pride at being in a wheelchair. There is probably some truth in this, especially as regards the early years. The writer once spent a fortnight with two young men newly disabled. I experienced their negative self-image, which was in marked contrast to my own view of myself and that of the other disabled young people there. While the rest of us were full of hope for the future, with talk of exam results and career prospects, our two sad friends had only nostalgia for the past when they were on their feet. I do not think Liam Maguire's anger was of this nature. His was the same anger as Martin Luther King's, the same as Gandhi's, the same as Jim Larkin's during the industrial unrest in Dublin in 1913, and the same anger as any social leader fighting for a segment of society with whom he identifies and whom he sees as being put in the role of second-class citizens.

It was in these years, the middle to late 1960s, that this writer came in contact with the IWA. For me, who had spent my childhood in a residential special school for those with cerebral palsy, the Association meant the assertion of my dignity and self-confidence in my own independent thoughts. Nobody expressed this better than Liam Maguire. At one particular AGM in the Royal Dublin Society, he was at his most eloquent. I recall snatches of his speech as he cried that it was not enough that disabled people be taken from their "hovels" once a month or a once a week for a special treat. He wanted disabled people to be able to move about as freely as anyone else in society. I was stirred and, perhaps for the first time, I felt a defiant pride in what I am, as I sat listening to Maguire's voice rebounding off the walls like water boiling in a pressure cooker. In future I was to be disappointed and very depressed at failing to do certain things, but I never felt the need to be non-disabled from this period onwards. Unfortunately research has failed to locate this particular speech of Liam's. It probably flowed from him impromptu, but he was to return to the theme again and again in later years, particularly in *A Fair Deal For The Handicapped*, which the IWA published in pamphlet form in 1977.

From the 1967 survey the Association went more and more into social services; employing more social workers and occupational therapists. The treasurer of that time, Seamus O'Seacoin, was very nervous about this, fearing that the Association would go broke. "Too often, says Fr Paddy Lewis, "we were hearing, 'we can't afford to do this, we can't afford to do that.'" Despite this the Association forged ahead in its new direction, and also in 1967 the Association's driving school was started.

It was that year, 1967, and on the question of mobility for disabled people that Liam made his first major impact. On July 6 he was summonsed to Dun Laoghaire Court for the non-payment of car-tax.

His father tells a story which captures in essence the tough determination of Liam Maguire. Bill Maguire wanted to accompany his son to help carry him up the steps.

"No, Da," Liam replied. "If they want me in that court they will have to carry me themselves." The *Evening Press* of that day carried a large picture of two policemen making a hard job of carrying Liam up the steps of Dun Laoghaire courthouse.

In court the arresting officer said that after he had questioned Maguire on 28 February he later saw that he still refused to pay tax and so had to make the summons.

Liam argued that for a disabled person his car is his legs. He said that without a car the disabled person has no chance of gainful employment as it is impossible for him to travel to work on public transport. He pointed out that as well as for his own mental health it was important for the economy of the state that the disabled person should be employed.

He proclaimed that three-wheeler invalid cars, which he said were given as "rejects" by the government in Britain, were mechanically unreliable, costly to maintain, unsuitable for medium or long-distance driving, anti-social as they seated just the driver, and unsightly because it was immediately recognisable that the driver was disabled.

That day Justice Herman Good's sympathies were all with Liam, but the judge had to enforce the law as he found it. Liam was fined forty-eight pounds, fifteen shillings, which Justice Good mitigated to one pound with a month to pay.

The car tax campaign contains all the qualities Liam was to show in the future. It lasted three years, during which time he put questions to the Dail mainly through David Andrews TD and also Sean Dunne TD, and had two meetings with Kevin Boland, then Minister for Local Government.

Disabled drivers were exempted from road tax in the 1968 Finance Act. This was followed in later years by relief from petrol duty, tax deducted from the price of a new car, plus a substantial car grant from local government. In 1967 there were fewer than twenty disabled people in Ireland driving their own cars. Since then that figure has jumped to the hundreds. Phil O' Meachair has said some of the credit for these statistics must go to Liam Maguire. The milkman's son had won his first major battle on behalf of disabled people.

To say that this victory changed Maguire would be an overstatement, but perhaps it showed him the road to follow, a way forward he had been desperately searching for up till then. Oliver Murphy, who admits that he hadn't liked Liam, said in reference to the court case, "after that I began coming round to him." He speaks about Liam's ability to go to the highest level in government and be treated as an equal. "They wouldn't be talking down to him— Liam would be talking to them eye-to-eye."

Chapter 5

In 1965 Liam was first elected shop steward by his Aer Lingus colleagues for his union, the Federated Workers' Union of Ireland. There were vacancies for three shop stewards, and his would have needed approximately 900 votes. Surely his election was significant in Ireland at that time, but those we spoke to say the fact of his disability was irrelevant. They say it was very obvious that he had the knowledge and ability to meet the task. Gerry Monks and Joe McGrane, both of whom served periods as WUI branch secretaries during the sixties, talk of Maguire as being somewhat disruptive as far as the management was concerned. Monks says there was a lot of tugging of the forelock in the presence of supervisors which Maguire refused to conform to.

We must see this in the context of the life Liam was living at that time. He was a thorn in the side of the Irish Wheelchair Association's board of management. He was beginning his struggle to have disabled drivers exempted from road tax. He frequented the pubs of Donnybrook where he met his artistic friends such as Eoghan Harris and Bob Quinn who were having their own political struggle within RTE. At night he could be found in places such as Groome's Hotel discussing socialism with Luke Kelly (of the Dubliners), who was a socialist, and Ulick O'Connor, who is not. O'Connor writes of having ferocious arguments with him into the early hours. Undoubtedly some of the workers he represented would have thought Liam too intellectual, and his ideas up in the air. He would have dismissed their views as ignorance.

Asked if the supervisors saw Maguire as a troublemaker, Joe McGrane says yes, "but the thing that I find unsatisfactory is that some of those supervisors would have seen any good effective shop steward as a troublemaker." McGrane goes on to say that Maguire "was a particularly tough negotiator and tough-minded person."

The author's intentions for this chapter are to establish that Maguire conducted union business, and worked for the members in a way that was unaffected by his disability. Paul Boushell, who worked alongside Liam for many years, says he was no ordinary shop steward: "anything but," Boushell retorts at the suggestion.

Boushell himself joined Aer Lingus in 1962. He says that in 1963 he heard of this fellow who had had a bad accident. "There was a collection to buy him a car, or to help towards buying him a car. There were things like that, but I didn't know him at all."

Paul Boushell says that in 1965 he would have been a shop steward himself. He qualifies his statement that Maguire was no ordinary shop steward by stating that it had nothing to do with his being in a wheelchair. "He was very forceful, even arrogant." Some of this arrogance showed itself to Labour politician, Micheal O'Halloran. When the two first met O'Halloran was running a course for shop stewards in Aer Lingus, and Maguire was rather cynical about the man sent by head office. O'Halloran says that at that time Maguire was full of energy but had little discipline, was critical of establishment but without any answers as to how things should be done.

Paul Boushell explains: "normally a shop steward serves a kind of apprenticeship. He started off with a bang! When Liam was shop steward, he was shop steward and that was it." He says that Maguire made a lot of friends and a lot of enemies very quickly because of his inability to suffer fools gladly. "His political views influenced him very much in his trade union activity," says Frank O'Malley, at present a branch secretary of the FWUI. "He was able to see things in a wider context. Whereas a normal shop steward will deal with whatever issue is happening on the ground; the significance of it generally or within the trade union movement as a whole wouldn't have had great priority. But with Liam, yes."

The state-sponsored body is a phenomenon almost unique to Ireland. Garret Fitzgerald described these bodies as "autonomous public bodies other than universities or university colleges, which are neither temporary in character nor purely advisory in their function, most of whose staff are not civil servants, and to whose board or council the government, or ministers in the government, appoint directors, council members etc." State-sponsored companies such as Aer Lingus are managed in a way similar to private enterprise with the safety net of state subsidies. As a socialist Liam would have approved, and felt a great affinity with Aer Lingus as a shining example of state enterprise. However, to seek a subsidy gives a bad public image and to return a surplus is considered success. Thus those in management view their as role similar to that of a private company. Liam would not agree, and this explains his catch phrase: "Aer Lingus is not David Kennedy and Company Limited."

Paul Boushell says that industrial democracy in Aer Lingus is well ahead of its time, largely because of Maguire. In 1974 Liam wrote a paper on industrial democracy, running to more than three and a half pages of closely typed script, which Paul Boushell speaks of as a classic. This piece follows very closely a theme later to emerge in *The Irish Industrial Revolution* and other publications of the Workers' Party. Maguire sees the benefits of worker-participation in the decision making process as: "Job satisfaction, the control of the enterprise, the formulation of policy, and the elimination of wasteful practices and duplication at management and other levels." He goes on to criticise the Minister of Labour for the proposal to have one third of the board "elected from and by the workforce." Maguire writes: "Surely anything less than a majority is tokenism." For Liam the long-term objective "shall be to work for the establishment of workers' democracy as an effective principle in Irish economic life: the public ownership of the means of production, distribution and exchange. We believe that the establishing of workers' democracy should be furthered by appropriate educational programmes. We believe that in addition to its own activities the ICTU should promote such programmes by establishing its own school or college of industrial relations."

The story of Liam Maguire, shop steward, seems inextricably linked with the trials and tribulations of Aer Lingus clerical workers over twelve years. Joe McGrane says that when he joined the airline in 1967, the clerical staff had a preferential position and he was unpopular because "I was seen as giving undue attention to the manual grades." McGrane felt that at that time the affairs of the manual workers had been neglected. However, by the early seventies, it appears that the situation had gradually reversed itself. Frank O'Malley explains that from the 1966 period the tradesmen and operatives had an agreement which tied their rates of pay to clerical rates, but the relativity was not reciprocal. Liam Maguire's view was that the clerks' pay was slipping relative to the tradesmen's.

Paul Boushell remembers the 1974 strike, which he says people are inclined to forget because it didn't last very long. There had been a national agreement that year and Aer Lingus had agreed to pay its tradesmen and general operatives a certain sum over and above this. When the clerks looked for their share of this extra money "they were told the cupboard was bare." The clerks then had a ballot, and on 30 August the strike committee issued a statement that the dispute was on behalf of all clerical, stenographic and allied grades and that the claim for parity with technical supervisors went back to 1968.

Paul Boushell says that management never thought the clerks would strike, and the clerks who voted for strike did not think management would push them that far. It was the first official strike in the airport and it aroused a lot of bitterness. Maguire was a member of the strike committee. Boushell: "We negotiated all day Friday; we were here very early in the morning. Meetings went on all through the night without Liam getting out of the wheelchair." There was a strike settlement around ten o'clock on Saturday morning, and Boushell says: "I think it was my stupid idea that we should all go to the hotel and have a drink before we went home to bed."

However, according to Boushell, one of the management team had left the meeting during the night and issued a statement from the Aer Lingus press office saying that the strike was over. "That led to a lot of problems for us," says Boushell, "because our people were on picket duty at the Airport, in O'Connell Street, in Grafton Street, in Dun Laoghaire and in Cork." The statement went out on the late news and people walked up to picketers saying the strike was over and asking why they were picketing. Liam and the other union negotiators knew nothing of this until Liam himself went to inform people in booking offices away from the airport of the real agreement. "The very first place he got to," says Paul Boushell, "he realised it had been on the radio." Maguire phoned Boushell in the hotel where the latter was still having a social drink with members of management. An argument erupted in the hotel. "They had agreed there would be no statement, and here was a statement. We broke into two sides again," says Boushell. "They presumably went home and we considered what we'd do."

The strike committee agreed to meet on Sunday. There was another shock in store as each of them bought the evening papers on the way home. Boushell says the *Evening Herald* ran a statement from Mr David Kennedy "congratulating and thanking all the scabs who had worked during the strike, even though it was just a few brief hours." Boushell says Maguire lost his reason over this.

When the committee met on Sunday they decided they had the right to re-impose the strike since in their view management had broken the pact. Management, having said publicly that the strike was over, were now under an awful lot of pressure, according to Paul Boushell.

Boushell says the two sides came together the following day in an acrimonious meeting. He says the management got sorry because the row had been their fault and someone said to Maguire in a sympathetic voice, "It's terrible Liam, we were all tired, but there you were sitting in your wheelchair all that time and we never gave you any thought or consideration." Given the mood of the meeting Maguire must have felt this to be very patronising and that he was being singled out as being different from the other strikers who (in the mind of the speaker)deserved no sympathy. Rejecting all pity, he replied: "Ah well, as I always say, it's better to be paralysed from the waist down than from the neck up."

At that meeting, Paul Boushell says, the company "bled money across the table. And we [in our inexperience] bled them for more and more and more." Boushell feels that Maguire would agree it was a mistake to negotiate though the night because when people get so tired they don't fully realise the implications of what is being agreed. He says that after the final settlement in 1974 there was a sense of unfinished business.

The dispute did not resolve the real problem of the relativity situation and so the settlement cost the company more than had been initially realised. All other groups were awarded the same amount the clerks got from the strike. The unions took the attitude that the settlement must be met regardless of cost.

This was the period of the mid-seventies oil crisis when, as well as huge increases in its wage bill, Aer

Lingus were faced with massive hikes in fuel costs. Management tried to retrieve the situation with cutbacks in overtime, shift work and staff recruitment. Some of the cutbacks were in areas where increases had been negotiated during the strike. Of course Liam and his fellow trade unionists were extremely angry at this. Frank O'Malley says that Maguire played a very intensive role during the period 1974 to 1978.

On 14 March 1978 the *Irish Independent* reports: "Peace attempts in the Aer Lingus clerical officers' dispute which has gone on for nearly thirteen successive hours broke down at two a.m. today and the airline now faces a crippling strike from noon today." The *Independent* goes on to report Mr Brian Hoey, then WUI Branch Secretary, as saying the company continued its refusal to negotiate on the union's well-founded 1976 claim for a substantial improvement in pay and conditions. According to Frank O'Malley, the 1978 strike was destined to be a lengthy dispute from the start because the management side feared if a settlement came too quickly it would be a repeat of 1974. Conversely the clerks' view that there would not be a strike was reinforced by the 1974 experience when they threatened strike and the dispute was over within three days with a lot of money crossing the table.

This misreading by both sides of the other's position meant that the 1978 strike was to be a long and bitter dispute. We have been told that Aer Lingus' chief executive, Mr David Kennedy, saw Liam as one of a hard core who were leading the clerks down a road they didn't want to travel. Conversely, it is said by one union source, once the strikers saw the efforts management were making to keep the company going without disruption, compared to the lack of effort to settle grievances, they became more determined.

Labour Court talks on the night of 14 March broke down; there was to be a full formal investigation the following Monday. Frank O'Malley says the union sent in a ninety-two page submission "and Liam Maguire nearly drove us around the bloody twist correcting the English; putting in the dots and commas, and getting the syntax right." Paul Boushell also talked about Maguire's exactness about the English language and his "nit-picking" at a letter that everybody else thought was adequate. Boushell talks humorously, as a man who appreciates what Maguire was about. For Maguire what was put on record was sacrosanct; a document must not be open to any ambiguity ten years after being written. Undoubtedly there were those who lost their patience, and Paul Boushell says a common cry was: "It's Maguire again! He's always at bloody things like that."

On 15 April 1978 Dr Charles McCarthy, Professor of Industrial Relations at the University of Dublin, was agreed as mediator in the Aer Lingus dispute. Over the next six days intensive meetings took place, culminating in a peace formula which was rejected by the strikers. Frank O'Malley talked about meetings lasting from eleven a.m. till seven the following morning with few breaks in between. "There was much coming and going with Professor McCarthy leaving to give lectures and coming back again."

The strike continued for another three weeks with Professor McCarthy acting as mediator. Then the strike committee was informed that a settlement had been put to the Minister for Finance and it depended whether the Minister was prepared to accept it. Paul Boushell says: "Liam would be seen, quite correctly, as militant and left wing, which would lead people to believe he'd be the one who'd hold out for the highest settlement and the longest period of time. But as soon as he realised that the Taoiseach himself had his finger in our strike then he worked rapidly, along with others, for a settlement." Boushell says Maguire would not be afraid of a strike against the government: "he'd have a strike against God," but being a responsible negotiator he saw how unprepared the members were for such action.

The government had a five percent barrier beyond which they were not going to go. The clerks received £450 each and a four-and-half percent increase in pay, plus a half percent in lieu of one day's annual leave being worked without pay by each employee before his or her retirement date. Frank O'Malley describes it as a "sham measure" and says he was not subsequently aware of anybody being asked to give up a day's leave.

After 1978 Liam got involved in his union at executive level. His activities at branch level became fewer and fewer. He was also made Disabled Passenger Specialist by Aer Lingus. Martin Dully, then Sales Manager in Aer Lingus says Liam did not "take the King's shilling," but whoever prepared this particular fishing rod had exactly the right bait.

Chapter 6

Jack Kerrigan and Oliver Murphy talk of Liam advocating at one period that the IWA ought to be controlled completely by people in wheelchairs, and that able-bodied people should be pushed out. Fr Paddy Lewis thinks that it was around this time there was a decision that the doctors—referred to as "technical members"—should become permanent members of the board; "so that the IWA (this is kind of ironic)—could not be taken over by the wheelchair members—Liam and company—and the money dispersed on purposes other than those for which it was gathered, that is this famous, or infamous, hostel."

Paddy Lewis says that for a long time Maguire was seen as a kind of threat as far as the Association was concerned. "But at the same time," Lewis continues, "he was doing very valuable work; about the taxation business for cars, and building up contacts with various people in government and public life." Lewis makes it plain that at the same time they were made aware that it was Liam doing his thing, and they were Liam's contacts. "However," he points out, "the job was being done and results were coming out of it. We all benefited from being able to buy a car without taxation and so on."

Although it was he who encouraged Liam into the IWA, Fr Paddy Lewis says; "He wasn't exactly what you would call a team player." Phil

O'Meachair proclaims: "He was an organisation man. But," O'Meachair delights in the contradiction, "that doesn't mean he wouldn't do his own thing outside the organisation." Lewis illustrates Maguire's tendency to go his own way by recounting an incident when television presenter, Bunny Carr, decided to have the Association on one of his programmes. Lewis says the group had done a lot of "pre-programme discussion" in IWA headquarters, but when they arrived at the studios, Liam was already there. The newcomers were then briefed on what was to be the format for the programme. "The lead in," says Lewis, "was Liam being his usual abrasive self, and talking about people helping; how that annoyed him." He says Bunny Carr encouraged this for the sake of good television. It was not the image the others had wanted to portray, and they were displeased at Liam's actions. Lewis says the day was a disaster and the programme was never shown on television.

Lewis says he wanted Liam in the organisation in order to harness his drive for the IWA's benefit. "He had that energy about him, whatever the source." Lewis talks about wanting this drive for the future development of the Association. "But also," the priest confesses duplicity, "I preferred to have him inside shouting out than outside shouting in at us."

As it entered its tenth year, the Irish Wheelchair Association was well established. It had had a stormy childhood with people of different views trying to pull it in different directions.

By the year 1970 those who advocated that the Irish Wheelchair Association should be a social services organisation—providing social outlets for wheelchair users, enabling them to be mobile with the establishment of a driving school and enouraging them towards paid employment—rather than build a hostel to facilitate medical treatment had won the day.

Bringing members on holidays was a very important function of the Association; for the young and the more severely handicapped it still is. Fr Paddy Lewis says: "The holidays brought people out of their homes from all round the country, and brought the holiday to different towns." He says the people of the town where a wheelchair holiday took place were woken up "to the fact that there were people in wheelchairs in the country, that people in wheelchairs could enjoy themselves, and would enjoy themselves, given the opportunity." He also points out that wheelchair users living in that town "got their first look at what could be done." Lewis says the holidays did much to help the expansion of the IWA afterwards, but can only remember one or two country committees being established as a result of holidays.

The author can verify Lewis's comments from personal experiences in Kilkenny in 1969. A group of young people around my own age on holidays from school began to frequent the place we were staying. They didn't become involved as helpers; seemingly they were just seeking company. They attached themselve to two to or three of us wheelchair users. We went on few of the official holiday trips; we just lazily rambled around the town as young people do. One day we went to one of the girls' houses where we listened to pop music; the Beatles, the Rolling Stones, and I think the Kinks were popular that year. The girl's father came in and I was talking to him about sport. I was dragged outside the door in the middle of that conversation, whether I wanted to come or not. We were off, up town to a restaurant which had a jukebox. On another occasion I remember discussing with one of the locals the merits and demerits of short story writer Frank O'Connor whom I had just discovered. As Fr Lewis points out, it was probably an education to some of these people to discover that a person in a wheelchair can be interested in the same things as themselves.

However, the IWA had to take one more difficult step before it took on the constitutional shape it has today. Fr Lewis, who was then chairman, tells us that the change from a simple board of management to an elected national council and national executive occurred in 1970. "I had been going round the country for quite a while," says Lewis, "going to the local committees that had been set up, and helping to set up others. More and more I felt that the local country committees were feeling that they were being cut out by Dublin. That everything was happening in Dublin; the money that they raised in their area was going back up to Dublin and they weren't seeing anything of it back in their own areas, that they had no say in the running of the Association."

This developed in Lewis the view that the Association's structure ought to be broadened. He says that every time he put this forward at board meetings the reponse was negative. "Particularly by those who were now regarding themselves as the permanent board members" (doctors). "So when the Annual General Meeting came up I put a proposal before it that called upon me, and the board, to draw up a new constitution for the Association, and present it at a special meeting of the Association in June. That gave us six months to do it," says Lewis.

"I did this on my own initiative," he continues, "and it was taken very badly by quite a few members of the board. I think they felt, at this stage, that I was trying to take over the board and the Association, for my own purposes, and that I was using my collar, and my contacts with the country groups, to unseat them. I was accused of all sorts of things, and the board meetings after that general meeting were very hot and heavy."

Lewis felt that although the AGM had passed his proposal the board members were still stalling. "So I went to a relation of mine who was a lawyer and told him what I felt was needed in the Association, and he drew up a constitution using his legal knowledge so that it couldn't be blown from any legal angles." Fr Lewis says he was naive for thinking that the board would just read his draft constitution and pass it at the first presentation. The suspicions of him persisted, and the board discused the draft article by article, word for word. Lewis concedes that it was right for the board to do this, "but it was obvious that it was a storm guard tactic, and they would agree only under duress." He says he was aware of time going rapidly; "and the June deadline was coming closer and closer. I felt that they would have to meet that June deadline, and I said so."

The wheelchair priest continues his story by saying that he spent some time in hospital. In his absence the new constitution was let lie. It was into June, and Lewis felt the board was neglecting its duty, particularly to the general membership who had passed a resolution. Again he took matters into his own hands. He sent the constitution, with the amendments from the board, out to the general membership and, as chairman, called the general meeting. Like a cute politician Lewis than took a holiday in the west of Ireland: "because I expected something to hit the fan at this stage." When he returned, Lewis says he found something of a revolution on his hands. The board were very angry that he had called the general meeting, and sent the constitution to the general membership. He says up to the night of the general meeting many were ready to take the chairmanship away from him.

At the general meeting Lewis put a resolution to accept the constitution as it was. It needed sixty-six votes to be passed and got only sixty. The board's own resolution to accept the structure of the association as it was laid out in the constitution, but to defer the details till the AGM was passed. However, Lewis says he was relatively satisfied, because the basic structure had been accepted.

Talking of the period from June to the AGM in December, Lewis says quite frankly: "They were a bloody six months." He talks of having special meetings to discuss the constitution which were all fully attended. "There were all sorts of debates," he says, "even about stupid single words at times." However after many meetings and working through article by article, the constitution was finally ready to put to the AGM.

Phil O'Meachair talks of the change in the constitution in these terms: "The disabled were beginning to raise their heads. They were beginning to talk if you like. And suddenly some people were saying 'they can talk!' mock dismay, 'we'd better listen to what they're saying. We mightn't take too much notice of them but we'd better listen to what they're saying.' " O'Meachair points out that the decision to change the constitution was passed by one vote and that vote came from a young disabled woman. So for the first time the ordinary members of the Association from all over Ireland elected a national council which in turn elected a national executive. Phil O'Meachair says the 1970 constitution opened up the Association for people like Liam Maguire to come in and have an effective say in administration.

It appears to be impossible for any of the people the author has asked to put an exact date on when Liam really became part of the Association and was first elected to the council. Among his private papers which were made available to me are records and minutes of many IWA meetings. The earliest of these records is a council meeting dated 1 July 1972 in which Liam reported on the transport arrangements in Europe for the Association's paraplegic Olympic team. Also in July 1972 the Kilkenny Branch of the Association wanted to keep more of the funds that they collected within their branch. "Liam," writes Phil O'Meachair, "was intolerant of Kilkenny's approach because it would deprive 'central organisation—the source of all wisdom—'of vital resources." This is one incident O'Meachair uses to illustrate the centralist in Maguire. The following year the Association contemplated having its headquarters in Laytown off the Main Dublin/Drogheda road. Liam was not enthusiastic: "He was at heart 'a Dub.' So headquarters in Dublin!" O'Meachair writes.

During 1972 and 1973 Liam was also lobbying the Ministers of Finance and Local Government through his old friend David Andrews TD. From the Finance Minister he wanted remission of Value Added Tax from new cars for disabled people. He wanted the Minister for Local Goverment to ensure that the civic offices being built at the time be accessible to wheelchairs, and provision be made for the employment of blind telephonists. Certainly Liam would have seen these matters as within the scope of his IWA brief, but he consulted his colleagues in the Association very little.

In 1975 while Liam was the Association's chairman he campaigned, in co-operation with Phil O'Meachair, CEO and the Association's Public Relations Officer, for special parking facilities for disabled drivers. This campaign culminated in Liam being summonsed for illegal parking. In court, on July 19th 1976, he stated that one IWA member "had the most appalling difficulties" because he couldn't park near his place of work in Dublin's city centre. Again the intention on Liam's part was to be summonsed so that he could make a statement in court. Liam refused to pay the £2.00 fine and said he was prepared to spend seven days in jail. He communicated this to the Minister for Justice on the same day. Today disabled drivers have free parking, and can park in certain places where the general motorist cannot.

In the mid 1970s the IWA commisioned a major research project. Fr Paddy Lewis describes *The Dimensions of Need* as a kind of follow up to the first survey done in 1967, which "had yielded a good deal of information," but was somewhat out of date.

At that time sociologist Pauline Faughnan was lecturing in Unversity College Dublin while serving on the IWA executive in a voluntary capacity. She says the lack of information on the extent of need among Association members emerged consistently at meetings of the executive. She talks of the late nineteen sixties and early seventies as years of rapid expansion, when the Association was making a greater and greater variety of services available to its members.

Faughnan was granted a year's leave of absence from UCD to undertake the research project, which was not finalised and published until 1977. "It was a lot bigger and more comprehensive than had been initially envisaged and took an awful lot longer than expected," she says.

Fr Lewis is not aware that Liam had any influence in setting up *The Dimensions of Need* survey. He says it was mostly Phil O'Meachair and himself who felt the need. Pauline Faughnan seems to verify what Lewis says. She remembers Maguire being on the executive committee without being significantly involved in the start of her project. "But," she says, in the same sentence, "knowing Liam, he would have been very committed to the idea of getting information, because for Liam information was a God to a certain extent. For him it was power to have information collected." In all Liam's campaigns we can see the evidence of Pauline Faughnan's words.

Shane O'Hanlon, one of the country's top civil servants, who often faced Liam across the negotiating table, writes: "In the Spanish bullring, the unfortunate bull is first roused by the mounted picadors, then enraged by the dart-throwing banderillos before the time comes for his final confrontation with the matador. "

During the early and mid 1970s Liam and some of his fellow workers in the Irish Wheelchair Association and the National Rehabilitation Board had a sequence of meetings with high-ranking political figures—the then Tanaiste, Ministers, Ministers of State and TDs to press for public action to make conditions more tolerable for physically disabled persons. By the time his frustration with the lack of any positive progress was reaching breaking-point,

Liam was advised by the Minister for the Environment that his next move should be to get together with a senior officer in the Department who was responsible for a number of the matters at issue. O'Hanlon, the matador, was to be faced with El Toro Maguire.

"It did not work out that way in practice," says O'Hanlon:

> From the outset we found a good working rapport which developed and grew close until his untimely demise. If I had niggling doubts at the outset that I was being used by him as a Trojan horse to subvert the establishment, I soon disabused myself of the idea as an unworthy one. Liam was a shrewd tactician and a trenchant protagonist, but an entirely forthright man who would have scorned such a devious course.
>
> More than any other person representing the disabled with whom I came in contact at official level, I regarded Liam as a committed and effective campaigner and a cogent advocate.
>
> To convince politicians and civil servants that changes in official attitudes are overdue and that action should be taken involving the spending of taxpayers' money, a comprehensive brief is essential, backed up by an unshakable belief in the merits of the case. As a member of delegations, Liam always came armed with a battery of statistics and estimates and with information about what enlightened states elsewhere were doing. He had the ability to marshall his submissions and to counter arguments against them as a general would arrange his troops.

Yes, the author admits to a childlike excitement, upon first researching Maguire's methods. It was almost like discovering how Shakespeare went about constructing a play, or why studying anatomy enabled Leonardo de Vinci to produce great paintings.

The first chapter of Pauline Faughnan's *The Dimensions of Need* traces the trend away from purely voluntary organisations being concerned about those with serious disabilities and towards greater statutory involvement through the regional health boards first set up in 1970. This was a trend Liam Maguire very much favoured, because he was very conscious of dignity for disabled people but, as a socialist, he would have thought it did not begin to go far enough. Liam's address to the conference of the Union of Voluntary Organisations for the Handicapped in 1977, when he was IWA chairman, was published as *A Fair Deal For The Handicapped*. The opening paragraphs read:

> The question of a fair deal for the handicapped is one with which all decent, fair-minded, Christian, Irish liberals have had an intellectual flirtation for many years. We are unanimous in our approval of organisations and measures which benefit the handicapped and we are each associated with at least one of these organisations to which we give a certain amount of our time and money. Indeed, some of us give a great deal of our time and money to these organisations. In fact, some of us give virtually *all* our time and money to these organisations. "So?" some of you say, resentful to my tone, "Is it not a good thing that we spend some, a great deal or all of our time and money on these organisations?" The short answer to that question, Ladies and Gentlemen, is "No."
>
> It is not a good thing when the end becomes the means, when loyalty and dedication are directed towards an abstract called The Organisation. We speak with some authority here because the Irish Wheelchair Association has consistently stated in public that our objective is to become obsolete; to be no longer necessary in our society. We are not sure if it is entirely possible to be without all of our voluntary agencies but we should certainly strive to create the conditions within the State where they would not be absolutely essential. We are

fully aware that what we are saying will raise anger and resentment among some of you here present—but be warned, those of you who so feel have taken the path of charitable benevolence. A fair deal for the handicapped is not exclusively tea and biscuits on a Sunday afternoon, or a trip to the seaside once a year, or a few shillings to buy fags and a jar, or home visits once a week, or second hand clothes. Each and every one of these items certainly ameliorates the lot of the handicapped in a charitably benevolent way and we are not saying that these should cease, but we are saying that there has been an undue emphasis on the aspect of charitable benevolence at the expense of real and fundamental change in the social and economic conditions of the handicapped in this country. At the receiving end of this charitable benevolence is a human being, an individual who has been denied his *right* to be cherished equally as a child of the nation. And for those who have the capacity to work there is an even more frightening injustice—they have been denied the right to be gainfully employed and to be allowed to develop potential self-sufficiency to its maximum. They have been condemned to a position of total dependence—not dependence on the institutions of State but as a slave or a chattel, dependence on their peers—other fellowmen and women.

Ladies and Gentlemen, a fair deal for the handicapped means nothing less than a real and fundamental change in the social and economic conditions of the handicapped in this country.

A Fair Deal for the Handicapped is just over nine pages long and covers the whole range of issues concerning the handicapped. Liam Maguire's strongest words refer to the situation of those handicapped living in institutional care: "We do not intend to mince our words here. We wish to make the most vicious onslaught on those persons and institutions who pay lip service to the dignity of the individual, and then proceed to strip the individual of every last vestige of dignity and independence." He mentions: "Elderly handicapped are awoken at

5.00 a.m. winter and summer so that they may be washed before the night staff go off duty; the matron insists on a month's notice when we are taking one of our members out for the day and that member has to be back by 7.00 p.m."

If Liam Maguire's ability to wield words was his most powerful weapon, much of the ammunition—factual and statistical information—was provided by *The Dimensions of Need* survey and the National Economic and Social Council's report on planning services for the handicapped, of which Pauline Faughnan was also a co-author.

Faughnan says that when *The Dimensions of Need* was finally published Liam was very much involved in furthering it, "and quoted it widely." A laugh comes into her voice: "any hour of the day or night Liam Maguire would ring me up looking for factual information."

Given that the aim of rehabilitation should be to enable disabled individuals to live free and independent lives in the community, *The Dimensions of Need* came up with some damning statistics: 18.6% of members living in institutions which not only means that they are effectively cut off from any normal social contact, but many, as Liam said, would have no say in decisions affecting their lives as basic as what time to go to bed. A staggering 58.4% were unemployed at a time, as Pauline points out, when employment among able-bodied was at a high level. And just 5.1% were leading active social lives without depending on special outings organised by the Association.

Pauline Faughnan agrees that *The Dimensions of Need* changed the Association. "While there was always the stirrings of political involvement, it changed things because number one, it gave the necessary information, and number two—more importantly still—it focused people's attention on the fact that you can continue to intervene and meet short-term needs for ever; providing holidays, helping families, getting people out of their homes..." At that time the Association was spending large amounts of money on housing and car grants to individual members. However, Faugnan points out, once the Association started looking at its long-term aims "you are immediately into the whole political arena."

It is evident that Liam Maguire thought of the Irish Wheelchair Association as a consumer interest group furthering the interests of its members at a politcal level. But is it? Many of those who get involved as volunteers do so to help with holidays and the weekly or monthly social. They certainly don't see themselves as joining a civil rights organisation. At a national level the Association is, to some extent, politically active, with members of the executive meeting Government Ministers and heads of departments. But at a local level, among the branches, this activity is at a minimum. Pauline Faughnan feels the working groups set up within the Association after the publication of her report have been effective in formulating policy, but not so effective in acting upon that policy. She talks of a tension between immediate needs and long-term goals.

It is important to note here that from the early seventies Liam was making frequent trips abroad, meeting disabled people from places such as North America and the Scandinavian countries. As we will see, people in these countries make it clear that they view the cause of disabled people very much in political terms. Having met some of these people it

is easy to appreciate Liam's impatience at the lack
of political awareness among disabled Irish people.

Chapter 7

In 1972 Maria Cassidy entered Liam's life. Maria's account of their first meeting is rather humorous. She was on a night out with her sister and a friend. As the night wore on the friend encouraged them along to Groome's Hotel. In Groome's they were joined by, in Maria's words; "this curly-headed fellow who talked about Russia and communism." Maria felt in no state for a heavy intellectual conversation and told him so. The next thing Maria realised he was gone. She said to her sister: "God, did you ever see such a weird fella. He appears out of nowhere, he talks about Russia, and when you turn around he's gone. What's more, Anne, he takes his chair with him."

"Maria," Anne replied deprecatingly, "the guy is in a wheelchair."

Maria could only respond with an embarrassed "oh." She explains that Liam had been sitting opposite her and that his large broad-shouldered frame had prevented her seeing the wheelchair. Maguire returned, and wanted to drive Maria home. Anne wanted Maria to return with her because it was a rule in the Cassidy household that the girls should go out together and come home together. However, Anne hadn't a hope against Liam's determination.

Maria says she was expecting a three-wheeled invalid car, and wondered where she was going to sit. At this time Maguire would have had a Cortina,

Corsair or Granada; no way would he be caught dead in a three-wheeler. Maria was given the display of Liam hopping into the passenger side and quickly sliding over to the driver's seat. Maria told us that she dared not touch the wheelchair as Liam had folded it and pulled it in behind the front seats.

Maria was nursing in London at the time and when she went back there Liam phoned her several times. She said she was very impressed by this as not many people made long distance telephone calls at that time.

When Maria returned to Dublin she phoned Liam and asked could they have a night out. She was aware there were other women in his life at that time. Lee Dunne and Ulick O'Connor are just two of those who comment on Liam always being accompanied by an attractive girl. Maria says that what attracted her to Liam was his vitality "and he had a dynamic force about him." which she says anyone meeting him for the first time could not but be aware of.

She talked about her not having many friends in Dublin and Liam being part of a wide circle which centred around O'Donoghue's pub in Merrion Row, Groome's Hotel and the Dublin theatre scene. "And to be honest, I sort of tagged on to the end."

Asked about the difficulties of getting into places that had narrow doors and steps of stairs she says: "At that stage he had everything under control; the theatre people knew him. I was just sent in to ask the doorman could he open the door, that Liam was outside. The fire exit door was opened, and he knew where to sit in the theatre that would be accessible." The exception to this was the Gate theatre which has a considerable flight of stairs inside the entrance. Maria considered herself a reasonably quiet person. "But I had to develop the knack of going up and asking people 'If you have no trouble with your heart or back would you mind giving us a hand up the stairs please.' " Maria said Liam wouldn't be bothered what happened at the end of the night; "He would sit in the bar drinking while I'd have one eye out for any strong bodies left to help us back down the stairs. But it never seemed a problem to Liam; he always managed to get out one way or the other."

According to Maria her parents accepted her love of Liam without question. She acknowledges that this is unusual and says most people "view disabled people as a race apart." She says that her parents' reaction was, "that I was quite happy and content and my life was my own." She says the fact of Liam's disability did not matter to anyone. This was partly due to Liam's self-confidence and the way he could present himself. Ronnie Drew is just one person who said the wheelchair didn't seem to matter with Liam because he managed it so well. Maria says that in later life her father ended up in a wheelchair and Liam helped him cope. She says that the fact that he had known somebody in a wheelchair who lived life to the full was a great help to her father and being disabled himself did not come "as such a dramatic crash to him."

Asked whether her parents did not even question if this was what she really wanted, Maria says: "People tended to look at Liam and then look at the woman behind the wheelchair without realising that the woman in herself was a very strong character and very strong-minded. My parents knew this about me and it was a case of 'if that's what you want, off you go.' "

The author feels that there should be no need to

write this, but the fact is that in the public mind in Ireland Christy Brown, the famous author, was the only disabled person ever to get married. There are many paraplegics, and other disabled people living ordinary married lives, which includes having children, away from the glare of publicity. Although people who have suffered a break in their spinal cord have no sensation below the level of the injury that does not mean they can have no sex lives. It was explained to us that the feelings are still present in the memory, just as a person who loses a limb has phantom pains for the rest of their lives. Thus when the love situation develops the sexual organs respond involuntarily. It would be quite wrong to claim that your sexuality does not change when you become seriously disabled; in some cases the non-disabled woman has to play the active role, but that does not mean that you are incapable of satisfying a partner. Maria says; "In a lot of relationships, and not only with disabled people, full sexual intercourse comes way down the line." She argues that understanding and loving must come first.

The sexual relation was there with Liam and Maria, although not in what most people would call the normal sense. "He was a very sexual man," she says, "a very sexual man to look at, a very sexual man to be with, and just because you happen to be sitting in a wheelchair does not mean you lose that drive, or lose that emotion." Some of the most striking photographs of Liam appeared in the March 1976 edition of *Performance*, a magazine concerning the disabled and employment, published in the US. In these photographs he looks like any handsome young man talking intensely with every part of his powerful personality radiating from his eyes. Ulick O'Connor, himself a former rugby player, boxer and Irish pole-vault champion, wrote of Liam as one of the most vigorous people he knew, "with his superb head like that of a Roman statue." Maria argues that the incidence of divorce and marriage breakdown is evidence that non-disabled people cannot always cope in a sexual way.

Maria talked about it having taken some time for her to realise the depth of Liam's character, and their having many rows because she didn't see enough of him. His commitment to political change for disabled people meant that Liam was forever rushing to meetings, or to attend some business. Maria says because of this their relationship was probably more volatile than most. She recalls one instance when they were to meet and he was tied up in trade union negotiations. The following day was Maria's birthday and she said to her sister: "That's it. If he forgets my birthday that's the last straw." Maria went home and it was her sister who found the hotel Liam was in. She got him out of the meeting on the pretext of an urgent message and reminded him of Maria's birthday. The next day Maria was "totally delighted" when she got a bunch of roses. "And it wasn't until a year later that I realised it wasn't Liam who had remembered." Because she had a lively interest in politics and an appreciation of what Liam was about, Maria probably had more patience than most girls would have in a similar situation. She mentioned to us his efforts to persuade people that rehabilitation ought to be treated as a political issue.

She also talked about the difficulties of getting close to Liam because he was a proud man. She believes that in the early stages the feelings were stronger on her part than on his, and because of this, one night two or three years after they met

Liam wanted to finish the relationship. Maria says: "Maybe he was testing me," because she was an able-bodied woman and he was a man in a wheelchair. He was telling her; the door is open; take your freedom if you want. Maria didn't want to go and said she would be very upset. She says that from that day he changed, and their relationship became stronger.

Liam and Maria were an unconventional couple in many ways. When asked why they never got married she says they were typically Irish in the sense that "something just goes on and on." She talked about marriage not being important to her in any situation because she valued her independence. "Both of us were of the understanding that there was a commitment there—a very serious commitment—and a piece of paper wasn't needed to enforce it." Likewise on the question of children she says: "Maybe Liam and I were just lucky in our minds and outrattitudes," and points out that many relationships break down for the want of children. "Liam and I were together eleven years. There weren't going to be any children. It was discussed, but it didn't break us." They faced the fact that there would not be any children. "So what do you have?" she says, "You both have a loving relationship, you both have a caring relationship, and just build on it."

In her own way Maria is as tough minded as Liam was. Probably it was only going to be someone like her who would be able to cope with what he was. Many say that when it came to any sort of argument or discussion he had met his match in her. Liam's mother told us that Liam couldn't make Maria do anything that she didn't really want to do.

"I didn't plan to meet the likes of Liam," Maria

says, "but I knew I didn't want a serious relationship until I had done what I wanted to do with my life, and as it happened with Liam the two were combined. We both travelled quite a bit and I understood what he was trying to achieve, which was very important in his relationship with anybody."

When asked about the difference between Liam the public man and Liam the private person, Maria says he had a very soft nature which people might find hard to believe because he did not always let it show. She illustrates this by recounting a time when he returned home from a workshop on employment for the disabled where there was a group of very young disabled people. She said: "It really cracked him up: their questions about employment, about jobs, about the future. It also angered him a lot and not only because he didn't have the answers to their questions. But," she continues, "I think he just felt he was tough and he was arrogant enough to cope with that big world out there, but what was going to happen to these children who maybe wouldn't have the same push as him."

Performance magazine wrote of Liam being different with his family from what he was in the outside world. "Softer, more respectful. When his mother is there, especially, the tone changes, the sentences lose some of their more peppery phrases. Over dinner with his family he discusses the same topics as with his friends—the union, politics, news—but at home he listens more, talks less."

Chapter 8

During the time he was getting to know Maria, in the early to mid 1970s, Liam made two more friends, two people who joined him on the road to civil rights for disabled people. Harry Ellis became paralysed from the waist down (similar to Liam) when he fell from scaffolding in his place of work. Colm O'Doherty was even more severely disabled when he was knocked from his motorcycle. Ellis is to be counted among the six or eight people who got to know Maguire most intimately. The abiding image of Liam Maguire is of his being very methodical as he moved in political, trade union and legal circles in pursuit of civil rights for disabled people, but he also had a great zest for life and friends knew him not only as sociable but as a great wit.

Harry Ellis describes himself "as the quiet man behind Liam." His brain works very differently from the way Maguire's did. He says of himself, "I'm not one for attending long meetings. When something needs doing, I believe in getting stuck in and doing it." When Maguire would get frustrated over accessibility—no ramp here, no ramp there, narrow doorways here and huge flights of stairs there—Ellis would say: "Look Liam, you'll never get a flat world." Ellis is an administrator. For years he has worked in fund-raising and various other areas for the Irish Wheelchair Association. Maguire was a visionary, always thinking up schemes to advance his cause. Sometimes one such as Liam, no matter how methodical most of the time, reaches for too much too quickly. Ellis was one of those who could put a check on him.

Colm O'Doherty's entry to the Irish Wheelchair Association mirrors very closely Maguire's own entry almost ten years earlier, but on this occasion Maguire was playing the role Fr Paddy Lewis had played then. O'Doherty says he became aware of the IWA the same day he met Liam Maguire and Phil O'Meachair in 1971 and was determined not to get involved. He says the notion of coming to IWA headquarters and being in a room full of wheelchairs was repugnant. "When they were putting Humpty Dumpty back together again in the hospital," O'Docherty says, "I made a conscious decision that I would not let my life be determined and ruled by chairs and people in chairs. I had an offer to go to a friend of mine in Kenya, I knew Maguire was involved in airlines and wanted to know the feasibility." The two arranged to meet in a pub. "Your man was there," says O'Doherty, "and he was fucking and blinding all around him as usual, and I thought to myself 'Jaysus y'know this is interesting. There's a bit of spunk in your man.'" We gather from this that O'Doherty hadn't seen much potential in the disabled people he had known up till then. He continues: "We had a jar, and that was the start of a beautiful friendship."

During the succeeding years Colm O'Doherty tells us he went his own way: "I built my own life; went to college, got my degree and got married." He had practically no involvement in the IWA. However, the friendship with Maguire matured. "We shared a few political platforms because we were fellow travellers along the socialist road. We'd have a few jars and chat about the issues. Then 1980 was on us and '81 was the year of the disabled."

One day Maguire was in the offices of the National Rehabilitation Board, where O'Doherty's wife works. According to O'Doherty, he stopped her in the corridor and demanded; "Tell that fucking husband of yours to get involved, we need him. It's time he got off the frigging fence and did some fucking work. He's full of good ideas, but he's a lazy fucker. Tell him to get in."

O'Doherty calls this "the Summons from On High," and says he was co-opted on to the IWA 's national executive. "I wasn't asked, I was told," to go to Adare Manor in County Limerick where the Association was planning its activities for the following year.

When it was said to Harry Ellis that people have called Liam a smoked-salmon socialist, Ellis laughs. "There's no such thing as a socialist, and I've said it to Liam. Every socialist aspires to be a capitalist. Liam was a capitalist. Ideally he kind of believed in the socialist system, but he liked the good life. He liked going into a nice restaurant, and having a bloody good meal. He liked going out for a jar. He liked going to theatre and cinema. He liked travel."

Rory Maguire remembers when his brother first got a Cortina GXL 2 Litre. When Liam drove into the driveway for the first time Rory stood and admired; "It's a beautiful car, but what in the name of Christ do you want with a big car like that?"

"It's me," Liam replied with an expansive smile.

Phil O'Meachair, chief executive of the IWA, compares Liam with the Dublin writer, Brendan Behan, saying: "If he was a communist, he was his own form." Liam had his ideals and philosophies, but like every human being he seldom managed to live up to them. Phil O'Meachair's comment stands against those who would judge him too harshly. "Of all the chairpersons we've had," says O'Meachair, "Liam Maguire brought more problems of people before me than any other chairperson." O'Meachair says Liam's voice would come over the phone pleading for someone else: "Can you do something?" "He had an awareness of need—of social need outside the Association." O'Meachair makes the point that Liam knew one didn't have to be disabled for life not to be a bed of roses.

Shane O'Hanlon, who has previously been mentioned in connection with Liam's campaigns, also met Liam in the 1970s. They met on a purely professional basis and were meant to be antagonists. However, several people have remarked on the rapport that grew between these two.

When asked to give his impressions of Liam Maguire, O'Hanlon wrote:

Obviously, the more complex a man's personality is, the more difficult it is to crystallise one's own personal reactions to him. Liam Maguire probably regarded himself as an uncomplicated, single-minded young man and would undoubtedly have demolished a would-be psychoanalyst with a couple of terse and impolite sentences. How wrong he was. In truth, he was a man of many parts. Liam was a combination of anomalies. Always proud of his working class background, he could move unhibitedly as an equal—frequently as more than an intellectual peer—amongst the patricians. He could be reserved, indeed morose one instant and ebullient the next. Capable of icy wrath and cutting sarcasm, his was also a most compassionate soul, especially where the underprivileged were concerned. A citizen of the world, he was at heart as true blue a Dubliner as that other meteoric Jackeen, Brendan Behan, with whom he shared a Rabelaisian humour, broad as that of the great

Elizabethans or our own Brian Merriman, but equally unobjectionable for all its earthiness.

He and I should have been incompatibles. Bureaucrats, such as I was, were his compelling targets and he had his own incisive way of making the fact clear. The manner of our first encounter (and I use the word advisedly) could well have established a state of permanent hostility for other auguries were less than propitious.

When we first met, Liam was a handsome young man, physically vigorous, despite his handicaps and in retrospect, I feel at the height of his intellectual abilities. Relaxed, he was effervescent company, though these moments became regretfully and progressively rarer. Brown curls brimming over a broad forehead and deep set eyes—had fortune been kinder to him, it would not be difficult to visualise him as an earlier Liam Brady or Kevin Moran, or even an idol of Hill 16, like Jimmy Keaveney, with whom he had facial resemblances. Like the bould Jimmy, Liam was at his most relaxed when nursing a well-pulled pint, shortly to depart "down the hatch."

But for that accident which changed his whole life style, a hectic, hyper-active existence lay before him. Those of us who travelled as passengers in his car, quakingly aware that Ireland had been denied a potential Niki Lauder or Alan Prost, had some inkling what career a "whole" Liam Maguire might have carved out for himself.

Fate has its own inscrutable purposes. The crash which denied Liam a full and active life amongst his physical peers was to prove a tantalus that was to make people and not only in Ireland aware of the lot of the physically disabled within the community and was to move those in public authorities to ease the difficulties besetting these handicapped citizens.

I have heard Liam snort resentfully that he was only "half a man." Crippled his poor lower limbs were, but an explosive energy seems to have drained from them to give him an added intellectual brilliance in his campaign on behalf of fellow paraplegics and a steely determination to win every concession which he felt society owed them.

Shane O'Hanlon and Phil O'Meachair are just two people who mention Brendan Behan, the boisterous Dublin writer, in relation to Liam Maguire. Eoghan Harris, television producer-cum-playwright, says if Maguire hadn't been disabled he might have resembled Behan and become just another Dublin wit supporting the counter in various public houses. The comparison is interesting but not wholly accurate, given that Behan squandered his talents and might not have written anything substantial but for the enforced discipline of spending time in prison. Maguire was much more determined and self-disciplined in what he set out to do. If Brendan Behan had lived beyond the early 1960s it is almost certain that the two would have met because Liam moved and was accepted in the literary circles of Dublin.

Ronnie Drew describes Groome's Hotel as a place which was used by actors, and people in show business generally, where they could go when they were finished work because everywhere else was closed. "It was a place where you found out what way work was going; who was working, who wasn't working. Liam was there. Obviously I noticed he was in a wheelchair, but I didn't dream of asking him why."

The writer Ulick O'Connor, well known for expressing controversial views on television, also met Liam Maguire in Groome's Hotel. O'Connor says "Liam wasn't one of these fellows that would take to you immediately unless he decided you were worthwhile. I would talk to him but just because I was well-known meant nothing to Liam." Ulick O'Connor says that after a time Liam began to drive him home "at a desperate pace; you'd be terrified out of your life." O'Connor says when they got to his house and Liam stopped the car, they would start to argue about politics. "We were often out till four and five in the morning fighting, arguing about the source of capital and income, because he was a convinced Marxist. The only thing worse than a convinced Marxist is a convinced Catholic because neither will listen to what you're saying."

"Yes," writes Lee Dunne, "Liam knew them all and he made sure they knew him. This was just the way he was; nobody went asleep while Liam was there." He writes of Liam's love of theatre. "He came to Limerick with me to see my play *The Full Shilling* which opened the Theatre Festival there in 1972. We were in London together to see *The Shaughraun* at the Aldwych in 1968. Liam liked to be entertained, but his theatre taste ran to plays with social themes."

It seems Maguire was most intimate with Lee Dunne who writes: "Liam was very dogmatic. When he knew something he knew it, and as I am very like him in this we drove each other nuts from time to time. It was typical of the kind of meaningful love-hate thing that can happen between men. Liam and I were very close for many years even though I wouldn't see that much of him. He would then appear with another lovely girl and we would eat and drink and talk and laugh. We argued over books and plays and girls, but it was all part of an interesting relationship. Liam and I, over the years, knew several women that we both went out with and went to bed with. These females knew he and I were pals, and I never heard one of them speak of him as anything other than great company and considerate."

"He always had a pretty girl with him," says Ulick O'Connor. Antoinette Andrews, wife of politician David Andrews, remembers that he could be humorous about his relationship with girls. She recalls on one occasion a number of girls were talking to Liam. At one point he whispered to Antoinette: "The thing that fascinates me is that none of them know whether I can or I cannot."

Lee Dunne tells of a peace rally in Phoenix Park which he says would never have happened but for Liam and himself. The idea came from "a heap of other people who were vaguely connected with Sinn Fein or something (I don't really know but they were always talking like they would be running the country before long). Liam or I, or both of us together, got The Dubliners to agree to appear. Also Nigel Denver, a Scottish folk singer, and others I can't remember. This takes a bit of organising, and on the Saturday before the day it was to happen, Liam and I were out together organising the sound system. The others spent their time in McDaid's talking about how great it would be." Dunne goes on to say that this rally would not have taken place without Liam.

Lee Dunne recounts an incident which, perhaps more than the others, evokes the companionship between the two:

One of my abiding memories of Liam Maguire is a night during the 1968 Dublin Theatre Festival. That particular night we were coming out of the Festival Club, an after-hours joint, legal for the duration of the festival. To be honest I can't remember whether we'd been to a play or not. Liam was insisting on driving me home, telling me I was a fucking eejit to think of driving home. I told him to get away from me and we had a stupid row. Finally he took off in the wheelchair, flying, yelling at me to remind me I was seven different colours of eejit. I watched him tear down off the footpath in the wheelchair, cross the street and attempt to get up on the other path. Well, old man barleycorn was working well, and for the first time I'd ever seen it happen, the bould Maguire misjudged the step and went backwards in the chair. Need I tell you that he was going to get a hard time over this one.

'Lee, Lee!' He was calling my name and I stuttered up South King Street. As I got closer to him I began talking to an imaginary companion. I described my sober, upright, altruistic friend Liam Maguire while he, lying on his back, suggested that my parents ought to have married before I was born, and on into a variety of technicoloured etceteras.

Harry Ellis echoes many of Liam's socialist friends when he says Liam had acquaintances in the world of the theatre and the media with whom he cultivated a friendship for some long-term objective. "If he could actually get one of them to say a piece on stage about the rights of the disabled then that was a goal somewhere along the line."

Talking about making the TV documentary, *Why Don't They Shoot People,* Bob Quinn says that Liam would have made a good actor. Patrick Maguire relates an anecdote that illustrates the extrovert in his brother. They went to Sydney, Australia together where Liam had a contact (many say no matter where in the world he went he had a person to contact). On this occasion they failed to find Liam's friend in the airport and retired to the bar. Patrick says that within minutes the company had swollen to ten, with Liam telling jokes along with another man. Patrick makes it seem like table-tennis as one told a joke and the other had a punchline.

New Yorker Bernie Stone is quoted as saying that his native city wasn't the same when Maguire "breezed in." He talks about bringing Liam to a pub called The Lion's Head which is frequented by New

York writers who got to know Liam. Stone, himself a TV producer, talks about a four-way friendship which included London-based TV producer Ian Stuttard and screenwriter Ronald Graham. Stone says he first met Liam in England when Ian Stuttard made a film defending the IRA in Northern Ireland. Maguire was anti-IRA, and Stone says the two argued all night, with Stone mixing the drinks and trying to keep them apart until 4 a.m. when Stone went to bed. According to Bernie Stone, Maguire and Stuttard continued a heavy drinking session well into the next day. In his letter to the author Ian Stuttard opens with "my dear friend Liam," and ends "even if he was a stick."

Another New Yorker, Malachy McCourt, writes of meeting Liam in the early 1970s: "we expected a Francis of Assisi and instead were presented with a roaring Marxist..." There are similar stories not only from Dublin and different parts of America, but even from places like Japan.

Yes, many would say, Liam had a combination of intellectual brilliance and natural Dublin wit that made him good company in a pub so long as he was treated absolutely naturally. But, as every handicapped person knows, very often total strangers, from a preverted sense of kindness, approach and say sorrowfully "You'll be alright," or some such banal comment. This, to say the least, is disconcerting when all you want to do is have a normal conversation with your friends. Liam had his own ways of dealing with this, and always left the perpetrator on the losing side. One example of this, given to us by several friends: one day when he was emptying his leg bag in a gents toilet this person kept staring. Maguire was aware of being scrutinized, but said nothing until he was about to leave.

Then, with the perfect timing of a true wit, he turned to his examiner and said: "That's nothing, you'd want to see me with an erection."

Colm O'Doherty relates an incident that occurred when Maguire was in no humour for subleties. Maguire, O'Doherty and Harry Ellis were having a drink in Dublin's Gresham Hotel. A man, not exactly sober, approaches and puts an arm around Colm: "the usual 'does he take sugar in his tea' "says O'Doherty.

"I'll buy you a jar there, sir." O'Doherty mimics a drunken drawl.

"That's very nice of you," O'Doherty responds with restrained politeness as the three exchange knowing looks, "I'll have a jar providing you buy yer man there a large Cork gin and my other friend whatever he's having."

The drunk took fifty pence from his trouser pocket and dropped it in O'Doherty's lap where he couldn't pick it up. The coin lay like an actor on an empty stage. Moments passed.

Then, "Fucking insulting cunts!" Maguire threw the rebuff like an hand-grenade which exploded in the plushness of Dublin's top hotel, "That wouldn't buy the steam off me piss. If you want to buy a jar put your money where your mouth is."

Harry Ellis said, "Where have you been, man? That wouldn't buy a bottle of orange." And O'Doherty told the drunk to take his fifty pence and put it in the poorbox and let them buy him a drink. A lot of people might condemn Liam's reaction, but it's a measure of how strongly he felt that disabled people shouldn't be expected to accept this sort of treatment.

Chapter 9

In 1967 the government established the National
Rehabilitation Board to look to the needs of all
disabled people. Ten years later the then Minister
of Health appointed Liam Maguire to the Board of
Directors of the NRB. Liam was one of the first two
disabled people appointed to the Board; the other
was Des Kenny, then of the National League of the
Blind. Until then all the board members were
doctors and other professional people. 1n 1979
Liam reportedly said that two disabled people on a
board of twenty was an inadequate representation
and that he intended campaigning for changes.

Des Kenny pulls no punches when asked what he
remembers of being on the Board with Liam. He
says Liam or himself couldn't ask a question and get
a straight answer "but you were nearly asked why
do you want to know." In one conversation with the
author, Kenny makes it seem that they were
treated almost like children, with Maguire as
trouble-maker and a bad influence on Des. Kenny
says that Liam brought to the NRB a questioning of
the slow pace and predictable pattern of its activities.

Kenny's opinions cannot be easily dismissed as
not very well thought out. With a diploma in social
science, in 1980 he was appointed General Secretary to the Union of Voluntary Organisations for
the Handicapped, and in 1986 became Chief Execu-

tive Officer at the National Council for the Blind. Kenny is more reserved in his manner—if not in his actual opinions—than Maguire.

However, to be fair to the NRB, Liam did have a crucial and productive role on its Access for the Disabled committee.

Access for the Disabled; Accessibility. What does it mean? Around Dublin and other cities in Ireland we are beginning to see ramps leading to the entrances of public buildings such as the National Concert Hall and the Mansion House. In the 1950s through the '60s and possibly up until the late '70s there was absolutely none of this. It wasn't seen as necessary. As Brian Malone points out, people with disabilities were not seen as needing, never mind making the effort to achieve, the normal things in life such as social contact with other human beings. Thus no provision was made for them to get into dance halls, cinemas, restaurants and public places generally.

Liam Maguire was just one of the several disabled people in the '60s and early '70s who was determined to change this. However, we can safely say that he was more uncompromising on the issue than most.

"He wanted to build an environment suitable for everyone," says John McCarthy, one of Liam's Aer Lingus colleagues. McCarthy is another trade union activist who was influenced by Liam to see the cause of disabled people in a political light. He recalls being on holiday with Liam in Spain. On arrival they discovered that Liam couldn't enter the bathroom. Maguire ordered that the door of the bathroom be taken down. McCarthy was standing on the toilet unscrewing the hinges when the bellboy returned with the luggage. The boy just dropped the cases and ran for the manager. But Liam was adamant and the door was taken down.

As Fr Lorcan O'Brien of the Irish Wheelchair Association says: "He was very conscious that the built environment as we have it, has in mind someone who is twenty or thirty, fully active, totally healthy, and carries no responsibilities or burdens." Outside that "totally healthy" group, Liam counted seventy five percent of the population including not only the disabled and the elderly, but people with illnesses such as heart complaints and respiratory problems, the mother pushing a pram, or even a person getting on a bus laden down with heavy parcels. Listening to some of Liam's speeches and various interviews on radio and television it is obvious that he wished, indeed willed, these people to unite in a political mass movement.

Tom Page, Administrative Assistant of the NRB, worked closely with Liam on the Access for the Disabled committee. As often happened with people who worked with Maguire, Page was a totally different character to Liam, but the two became very close. Tom Page is a tall grey-haired man with a pleasant conversational tone. A gentle character, his commitment is without the rough edge there was to Maguire.

Page recalls a time when he was in hospital and Liam paid him a visit.

"He just rolled up to the bed beside me and said, 'How're ya Page?' " The macho Dub.

"Ah Liam, how are you?"

" 'Ah,' said he, 'Great.' "

"So we were chatting and talking for ages," Page says. "And he was in good form, cod acting with the nurses. He gave me a present of a Hugh Leonard book."

This is just one of the anecdotes Tom Page used to illustrate that "behind all the brashness and the roughness there was a sensitive guy. If he was painted all rough and aggressive he wouldn't be the real Liam Maguire at all."

Tom Page told us he himself took the attitude that he could get more from people by gentle persuasion. He would write to people who were developing or owned a shopping centre asking them to provide car parking facilities for disabled drivers near the entrance.

Dun Laoghaire Shopping Centre was one of the establishments that granted this request, and allotted two parking spaces next to the entrance. The international access symbol was painted on the ground in both of these parking spaces.

"Despite this," says Page, "every time Liam went out there, both the parking bays were occupied by some so-and-sos who were not disabled. Maguire got so fed up with this occurrence that one day he parked his own car across the rear of both cars in the special parking places making sure to block them in. Liam left his car and probably visited a few of the local pubs," says Page. "He deliberately stayed away a long time and the two car owners had called the police who in turn told them they should not have parked there because it was reserved for disabled drivers only. However their anger had not abated by the time Liam returned."

"What are you fucking steaming about?" retorted Maguire. "They are my fucking parking bays."

"You had no right to park in front of us."

"Well, I couldn't park in there because you two had my parking space. You won't park there again."

"And they didn't," concludes Tom Page.

"We used that as a tactic," said Page. Sometimes he would ask Liam to approach people when he was getting nothing out of them by using his own methods. Other times it happened in reverse. "Quite often Liam would come and say,'I'm getting nowhere with this bloody crowd. Will you try?' And I'd hear a litany of complaints about this awful character Liam Maguire." He often felt that after coping with Liam people would co-operate with him for fear Maguire would come back at them.

Tom Page talked about Liam achieving things that others would not have the energy or the tenacity for. "He was such a strong-willed and dominant character that sometimes he built up a counteraction and people would dig in their heels and do nothing for him."

From here Page moves on to a meeting the committee had with the Department of the Environment. They were there to talk about access generally and Page thinks they were making representations about the Draft Building Regulations. They were all being sociable before the meeting, which couldn't start without Liam Maguire.

He was fifteen minutes late. They were about to start the meeting without him when a porter came running in the door saying there was a man in a wheelchair down on the fifth floor and he wouldn't come up any further. "I was regarded as one of those who could handle Liam," continues Page. "So I went down to him and said 'Liam, we're up on the eleventh floor, so c'mon and we'll go up to the meeting.' "

"No! I'm not going up there," said Liam. "That lift is supposed to be capable of being used by a wheelchair user and I can't reach any higher than the fifth floor button, so I'm not going any higher than the fifth floor." He refused point blank to budge.

Tom pleaded with Liam and told him he had made his point, but Maguire remained adamant.

Finally forty-five minutes after the appointed time the meeting was moved down to the fifth floor, only for people to discover that the corridor was half taken up with parcels of stationery which had to be moved to allow the wheelchair to get by.

When he talks about the Board's "Minimum Design Criteria" the NRB's Assistant Administrator illustrates Liam's strong views and his determination to express them whenever and wherever he felt the need to. In the early '70s the Board got students in the College of Occupational Therapy to survey three hundred buildings in Dublin and produced a guidebook called *Dublin for the Disabled*.

Tom Page says that every city in Europe and America had produced such a guide and *Dublin for the Disabled* was highly thought of when it was published.

By the time Liam joined the Board, the first edition of *Dublin for the Disabled* was running out. It was time to reprint. The question was whether to do another survey or just reprint what existed already.

However, Liam Maguire spoke. "What the hell is the point in producing a guide to Dublin for the disabled when all you are telling them is that there are twenty-nine steps to the Custom House and they can't get in, and there are eleven steps to such and such a place and you can't get in there. There isn't a building in Dublin that you can get into."

"He was very strong on this," Page remembers. He said there was no point in producing it: 'You're only codding yourselves and codding the people who think it's a lovely publication. That's not taking away from what Tom Page has done; but it's a waste of time, it's no good to the disabled at all because all it tells you is that you have no business being disabled in Dublin."

"Why don't you try and change the city? Why don't you make the city accessible?" There was such logic in his argument, Tom Page tells us, that the committee had to agree. It was decided to promote the International Symbol of Access.

Once the decision to promote the symbol was taken, the committee had to decide what standards would apply. Although the symbol is the copyright of Rehabilitation International it was found that there were no standards set down for its use. Page himself had visited France where he had seen the symbol on doors at the top of a flight of stairs!

Liam kept up the pressure. His attitude was, that in the absence of international standards, it was up to the National Rehabilitation Board to produce standards. Thus, they began work on a fourteen page document called "Minimum Design Criteria."

The document sets the standard not only for ramps and minimum widths of main entrances, but also specifies the interior dimensions of the building to allow the free circulation of the wheelchair-user. Corridors must be a minimum width of 1000 millimetres, and where there is more than one floor, a lift must be provided capable of carrying a wheelchair. It is essential also to have a toilet for the disabled which is not only wide enough to allow a wheelchair to enter through but gives space at the side to allow transfer from the wheelchair.

Tom Page talked about the efforts to develop a

suitable toilet for the disabled. Several plans were drawn up, redesigned, and scrapped until they decided the best solution was to forget about "Ladies" and "Gents" and just have a toilet for the disabled.

Dublin Corporation were beginning to build several such toilets around the city and Page remembers going to inspect two of them in the Crumlin area. He was accompanied by Liam and one or two others. He tells us it was a wet and dreary morning and as they approached the first toilet in Pearse Park they were greeted by three or four Corporation men whose features were in sympathy with the elements.

Reluctantly the Corporation men showed them the toilet which had been brutally vandalised. They then went to the other toilet in Stanaway Park and that was the same. "They must have used a sledgehammer," Page tells us. "At this time we reckoned on about two thousand pounds worth of damage."

Tom talks about being very upset and disheartened. "We went into a nearby pub and some of us had coffee and some of us had hot whiskies and others had two or three hot whiskies, because we were really depressed. We came out eventually to go home or back to work and we were really sick, saying what the hell is the use, it's a lousy bloody country and you can have nothing in it."

As they were gloomily departing from outside the pub and getting into cars, Page says his keys caught in the lining of his pocket. He was trying to fish them out without damaging his clothes. Eventually he found it was his AA key that caused the problem. "A bloody big long key and it suddenly struck me," says Page "the AA does that with telephones, and they are locked so nobody can get at them unless they have a key. I suddenly had a brainwave: why can't we do something like that with the toilets?

"So we all went back and had more hot whiskies, and after we discussed it and said 'Why not?' "

An idea was born; now a key to open all the special toilets is available to any disabled person who contacts the National Rehabilitation Board. Page tells me there are several such toilets in the city of Dublin and other towns around Ireland.

The Access for the Disabled movement, like any such campaign trying to bring about change, is often a process of taking two steps forward and one back in the hope that at some future time you will be able to take another two steps forward and one back.

In January 1979 Liam was concerned that a list of hotels providing only some degree of accessibility should not be given the status of official NRB accommodation.

This arose because the committee was involved in preparing a list for Bord Failte outlining the degree of accessibility in various hotels. "A lot thought him unreasonable," says Page, "but I think most people could see his point. Liam's argument always was that the international symbol stands for certain conditions in Ireland and those certain conditions are set down in the Board's Minimum Design Criteria and if the hotels or other places of accommodation don't meet with those criteria then they don't get the symbol and that's it."

Others argued if you stick too rigidly to that you would never get a hotel with the symbol because none of them quite meet the standards.

"Well, you will have to get some to meet it, said Liam, "before you start watering it down, because otherwise there is no point in pushing the symbol at all. Or there is no point in looking for access. What we are looking for is full access, independent access."

As far as Liam was concerned there was no reason on earth, technically or from the point of view of construction, why a place couldn't be made fully accessible, and there was no extra cost involved if it was done at the planning stage.

However, the committee in general felt they were getting nowhere and the same argument came up repeatedly. About six hundred registered accommodations had been circularised through Bord Failte and according to Tom Page, "there wasn't one single one of them that you could even feel was likely to be useful to anybody on the basis of our criteria—that is access without assistance from anybody."

Gradually the committee drifted towards the idea of two symbols. The international symbol would indicate that the premises was fully accessible and another symbol would indicate access with some assistance.

"Liam was half hearted about that," says Page, "but he wouldn't reject it. At that stage we were getting one or two places which were just about able to qualify for the symbol."

In the autumn of 1984, a year after Liam's death, the committee did their second survey with Bord Failte and found ten premises that qualified for the full symbol of accessibility and fifty that qualified for the second symbol of accessibility to the wheelchair user with assistance of one person.

Finally Tom Page talked about Liam's efforts to have accessible public telephones. The committee was trying for years to get the Post and Telegraphs to install a telephone for the deaf and Liam said they should have one for wheelchair users as well.

The Department of Posts and Telegraphs were slow-moving but after numerous letters and phone calls from Tom Page, they finally agreed to a meeting. Liam was one of those people Page brought with him to the meeting. It sounds like Noah's Ark as he lists the sections of the Post Office from which there were two representatives. "Despite all this," Page continues, "nothing happened."

Eventually they agreed upon the height of the shelf and the basic design. However, it was six months before the shelf was put in, and another six months after that, according to Tom Page, there was still nothing on it. Liam's anger was reaching a climax. He was contacting different people including the Post Office Workers' Union. As a result of that there was a telephone put on the shelf, but when he went to try it, it wasn't connected.

Again he got on to the union and they agreed to push it from their side. Tom Page remembers a heated argument upstairs in the GPO. Maguire decided there was only one solution. He said he was going to place a picket of wheelchair-users outside the GPO. Then "Hey presto," says Tom Page, "the job was done and the telephone installed." The attitude of the Post Office changed to one of understanding. With advice from Liam and Tom Page, they went on to develop a public telephone kiosk accessible to wheelchairs.

The episode with the Department of Posts and Telegraphs is an example of an occasion where Liam's aggression produced results. But it was not always the case, as we see in other chapters. There were those, even among disabled people, who disapproved of his methods.

It was not only on the NRB committee that Liam campaigned for accessibility. In October 1978 and again in July of the following year, Liam, as the Chairman of the Irish Wheelchair Association, was in contact with architect Sam Stephenson concerning accessibility in the Central Bank. On one occasion he produced an extra wheelchair and told Stephenson to try and go around the building in it. Some say it was the most broken-down wheelchair Liam could find and he let the air out of the tyres to make it even more difficult. But Sam talks about it in a serious manner. "It was a very practical way of dealing with the problem," he says, "because until you actually suddenly discover that you can't get up to walk around, it's not easy to understand the position. There were quite a number of things I just couldn't do and a number of doorways I couldn't get through." Sam Stephenson says that while Liam was a strong advocate of his position he was always reasonable. "There were some things the bank could not change at that stage and he accepted it."

Yet others say that Liam felt that Sam Stephenson, more than any other architect, should be aware of accessibility, having designed the Central Remedial Clinic in Clontarf and Colm O'Doherty remembers Liam criticising Stephenson in the Montague Hotel in Portlaoise.

Chapter 10

While Liam was campaigning on the rights of disabled people, being an effective shop steward, and living a hectic but interesting social life, he was also playing a part, some say a significant part, in the development of a new political party.

Starting with James Connolly, who founded the Irish Republican Socialist Party in 1896, socialism in Ireland has been mixed with, some might say diluted by, the nationalist cause. Connolly saw Irish independence as a prerequisite to establishing a Socialist Republic. Thus he joined with Sinn Fein—who were by no means socialists—and others to lead the Easter Rising of 1916. After his death, Connolly's socialist ideals were quickly watered down by the first Dail in 1919.

In June 1935 the journal of the Republican Congress, an organisation established in March 1932 by Frank Ryan, Peadar O'Donnell and other socialists, accused the IRA of attacking its own left-wing elements instead of using the economic war for the advancement of the socialist movement.

As Tim Pat Coogan points out in his book, *The IRA*, the development of all but two of the political parties in Ireland can be seen as the breaking away of the less radical elements from the revolutionaries; starting with Cumann na nGaedhal establishing the Free State government in 1922 which resulted in the split that caused civil war. Then in

1926 Eamon de Valera took the Oath of Allegiance and founded Fianna Fail. It could be said that in 1970 the split happened the other way, when the Andersonstown branch of Sinn Fein departed from the Official IRA This led to the establishment of the Provisional IRA which became the principal physical force movement in the North. The military wing of the Officials gradually died away, and Official Sinn Fein became Sinn Fein The Workers' Party.

On 21 September 1979 Liam Maguire wrote to Eamon Smullen, Sinn Fein The Workers' Party's Director of Economic Affairs: "As a non-public active member of the Workers' Party I wish to convey to you my disapproval of the continued retention of the prefix 'Sinn Fein' to the party name. There are no political advantages to be gained from this retention. Indeed there are distinct disadvantages when one considers that a large part of the general public is unable to distinguish between the two Sinn Fein parties. The disadvantage is not the possibility of the loss of votes but rather the damage which can be done, inadvertently or otherwise, by the media. We had a recent example, I am told, on the *Day by Day* programme where the compere, Pat Kenny, confused the parties, to our distinct disadvantage."

That letter continues: "It ill behoves a progressive industrial organisation which is presenting its policies on a platform of dialectics and economics to allow itself to be confused with a nationalist and fascist terrorist gang..." Strong words which tell us much about the make-up of Liam Maguire.

To attempt to understand Liam Maguire's political outlook we must see him in the general context of Irish politics in the 1970s, which were greatly influenced by the civil strife taking place in Northern Ireland. On 2 February 1972 the British Embassy in Dublin was burnt down during massive demonstrations to protest at thirteen people being shot dead in Derry by British troops three days earlier. Ulick O'Connor says that it was more than likely Maguire was there, but we can definitely say that Liam would have seen the actions of Bloody Sunday not simply as a British-Irish clash, but as an extreme example of the oppression of the working class by a conservative establishment. His girl friend, Maria Cassidy, remembers Maguire arguing with an IRA supporter in a north Dublin hotel against the shooting of British soldiers who would have come from working class areas in England, Wales and Scotland. Oliver Donoghue, who knew Liam very intimately for fifteen years, writes about Liam's readiness to change his views in the light of new information: "we both started out with a 'Republican' view of the Northern Ireland problem, but the lessons of the Provisional's campaign of terror against the Protestant majority made us rethink about the so called 'Six Counties.'" Donoghue says this "rethink" led them "to challenge the false assumptions of Catholic nationalism inside the working class and socialist movement." Donoghue talks about Maguire and himself moving away from the indoctrination of their childhood that the Roman Catholic people of the island of Ireland were one people and that the Protestants of the north were intruders put there by England from whom everything bad came. However this was also the developing view of liberal intellectuals such as Garret Fitzgerald and Conor Cruise O'Brien. For Liam and his friends the justification for this change of view would go back to the 1830s and

Daniel O'Connell, who was the hero of Catholic Emancipation in Ireland, but an opponent of trade unionism in the British House of Commons. This they could not have agreed with.

Whether Maguire would use words similar to Oliver Donoghue to express himself is impossible to tell. Interviews this author has done with Maguire suggest that he would. People like Oliver Donoghue and Eoghan Harris would want us to see him as an absolutely committed, even hard-line, socialist. Evidence suggests, however, that he would learn the art of compromise as quickly as any man when faced with the realities of power. Labour politician, Micheal O'Halloran says Liam would have been publicly critical of Labour in coalition with the conservative Fine Gael, but being a political realist privately would have accepted that there are times when only certain things could be done. A look at his career in the Irish Wheelchair Association gives us an insight. In the early days the leadership in the IWA saw Liam very much as a disruptive element. Then when he came on to the executive, Fr Paddy Lewis says, "he became very responsible." It has been said to this author that Liam Maguire made no objections when IWA staff didn't get pay rises due under National Agreements because money was scarce.

It is difficult to discover precisely what function Liam had in the Workers' Party. Even now, after his death, his friends are reluctant to talk about this issue. In his private papers, made available to the author, the letter quoted above is the only piece of concrete evidence that he was a party member. People like John McAdams, who served alongside him on the executive of the Federated Workers' Union of Ireland, say it didn't suit his position in the disabled people's or the trade union movements openly to admit membership of the party. Whatever about the field of trade unionism—those that come to prominence in the trade union movement usually have socialist leanings—certainly the majority of people involved in the IWA do not see themselves as being left wing. Yet Liam's membership of the Workers' Party was very much an open secret.

Throughout the 1970s, Sinn Fein The Workers' Party were struggling to be recognised as a respectable party of the left. It is reported that the change from a traditional republican message to a Marxist outlook stemmed from Cathal Goulding who avidly read revolutionary tracts while in prison in England between 1956 and 1962. As we researched for the purposes of this book, it appeared that as the party began to develop away from the violence of simple republicanism, it attracted people like Liam Maguire who advocated Marxist policies and had a very non-nationalist view of politics. However not all party members agreed with Liam, and the proposal to change the name was defeated at the 1980 annual conference by a vote of 60%. The prefix was dropped in 1982, and the name then became simply "The Workers' Party." But it is significant that the party President is still known as Proinsias De Rossa, the Irish version of his name.

The then Official Sinn Fein made its first moves towards influencing the trade union movement in 1972. Oliver Donoghue and Eoghan Harris—both close personal friends of Maguire's—were in contact with Cathal Goulding and the party leadership in general. Oliver Donoghue, who is mentioned in earlier chapters, is a training officer in the Irish Congress of Trade Unions, and playwright Eoghan Harris would have appealed to the intellectual in

Liam Maguire.

The May 1982 issue of *Magill* magazine reported that Sinn Fein the Workers' Party set up a new industrial section in 1973 under the directorship of Eamon Smullen. A significant number of members in this section would not be publicly associated with the party. Smullen, to whom they reported, was their only link with the party. Initially two "secret cumainn" were founded; one within the Irish Transport and General Workers' Union, and the other in Liam's union, the Workers' Union of Ireland.

Oliver Donoghue strongly denies that there was anything secret about the party's activities in the trade union movement. Donoghue says Liam had direct contact with the party leaders on matters concerning disabled people due to be discussed in Dail Eireann

According to *Magill* the ITGWU group was the strongest at the initial stage but it was shortly overshadowed by the WUI cumainn as "Smullen became more and more dependent on the Harris-Donoghue axis for research and policy." Maguire carried out much of this research. Eoghan Harris says because he travelled all over the world he could collect top information. Harris says Maguire would sit in "boring" company all night if he thought that when they were "well oiled" he would get some valuable information from them. The policy document on how the party was to increase its influence in the trade union movement, written by Eamon Smullen, lays stress on the importance of information such as "what profit a boss made last year and if that boss is a director of other companies." The policy document continues: "Workers soon understand that the party member can be depended upon to supply all sorts of information not readily available to the general public."

In 1974 the party published *The Great Irish Oil and Gas Robbery*. This booklet documents the growth of American oil empires such as the Rockefeller dynasty and how they came to dominate the exploration of Irish offshore oil. Chapter Four, "The Rockefellers Tell Yarns," quotes experts such as Dr Sean O'Donnell of Edinburgh University and Dr F Howitt of British Petroleum to support its argument that the oil industry is deliberately misleading the Irish public on the commercial potential of Irish offshore oil and gas. Oliver Donoghue says at least some of the information for this study came through Liam. We are told that he gathered this by talking to people he knew in America and read international business journals as source material. Also documented is the extent to which the oil barons are aided and abetted by the Irish business class. According to the study, Irish businessmen did this by taking directorships in twelve Irish petroleum royalty companies which are only fronts for American interests. The "Irish oil gombeens" are useful to the Americans because they are also directors of numerous other Irish companies, ranging from banking to newspapers and covering the whole spectrum of Irish industrial and political life. "The power at the disposal of this handful of wealthy men stretches into the life of every Irish working man and woman. They control wages and welfare. They control what people read and what people think."

Published in 1977, *The Irish Industrial Revolution* is known as the bible of The Workers' Party. In Chapter Five we see statistical information about American companies that might have come from

Liam Maguire.

"Liam was a deeply read man," Eoghan Harris writes, "who agreed with the party's theoretical line. This line changed so profoundly in the period 1972-79 that literally a new party was created: anti-nationalist, Marxist, democratic." Harris also writes: "Liam was a 'cadre,' that is an activist, a fighter, an implementer of policy on the ground, in unions, often by taking up issues which were not party issues but could be turned around."

Oliver Donoghue says that Maguire was one of the people very clearly identified with the beginnings of the PAYE campaign inside the trade union movement. "He was making speeches at ICTU and FWUI conferences about tax reform being a class issue." Donoghue says that, before this, a publican might boast to the labourers in his bar about dodging tax and the labourers would think the publican very clever. Donoghue contends that Liam made a major contribution toward the present climate where the labourers would now be angry that this wealthy publican should dodge paying his income tax. However, Bill Attley of the FWUI denies that Liam Maguire was a major influence in the PAYE campaign of the late 1970s.

At the annual delegate conference of the Federated Workers' Union of Ireland, Liam moved a resolution calling for "a land tax on all agricultural land in order to bring into cultivation the one-third of viable Irish land not being utilised by farmers at present." The tone of this speech very much reflects that of *The Irish Industrial Revolution*, which condemns Irish farmers for concentrating on pasture instead of dairying and tillage which provide more employment. Liam is critical of West of Ireland farmers failing to grow enough sugar beet for the state-owned Tuam Sugar Factory in county Galway, and reneging on potato contracts they had with the same Irish Sugar Company. He goes on to illustrate that Irish farmers have failed to achieve the land's potential for wool and timber production.

At the same conference Maguire calls for the abolition of the Common Agricultural Policy "which," he says, "cossets the inefficient and downright lazy, penalizes the taxpayer, starves the pensioner of meat and creates ridiculous community-use phrases like butter-mountains and wine-lakes."

Pat Rabbitte, formerly of the Irish Transport and General Workers' Union, (now a Workers' Party TD) says: "He identified with an analysis of modern day Irish society which says that the interest of the farming community is no longer identical with that of society as a whole."

At other conferences of the Irish Congress of Trade Unions, as well as the Workers' Union of Ireland, Liam spoke on the construction industry, the need to expand state enterprises, and moved a resolution calling for a 2% levy on all agricultural produce.

Bill Attley, a Labour Party member, says the trade union movement was critical of the farming community long before Liam Maguire and the Workers' Party. When this was put to Oliver Donoghue, he says that Liam and the Workers' Party advocated a policy beyond simply being favourable to small farmers and opposed to big farmers. "We would be in favour of the land being used for the benefit of the maximum number of people" and "challenging the notion that there was a basis for an alliance between small farmers and workers." This ties in with Pat Rabbitte saying that

Michael Davitt propounded the common ownership of the land before the Land League was hijacked by other political elements and turned into a campaign for peasant proprietorship. The Workers' Party would say that once the tenant farmers achieved ownership they became cne of the most conservative elements in society. This in turn coincides with Liam's criticisms of farmers in the west not supporting a state enterprise, the Irish Sugar Company. Maguire's anti-rural bias was so strong that Bob Quinn, who moved to the west of Ireland, says he often told Liam; "You are just another sloganeer."

On the question of the expansion of the public sector, a subject Liam spoke on at ICTU conferences in 1976 and '77, and nationalised industries, Oliver Donoghue says The Workers' Party would go further than the Labour Party. Donoghue argues that the Labour Party does not say the Irish Sugar Company should be the major food processing company in Ireland, or that the activities of Bord na Mona should be expanded into farming.

It is not our function here to assess the policies of the Workers' Party or the Labour Party. Rather it is to illustrate that because Liam talked about these issues and was concerned about the trade union movement generally he was able to convince his fellow trade unionists, even those who did not always agree with him, that as socialists they ought to take a more serious interest in disabled people.

Chapter 11

Liam saw himself as a socialist. We can safely say that Jim Larkin, that towering labour leader in the Dublin of 1913, was one of his heroes. Like Larkin he had a genuine concern for other people. However, in Larkin's day the socialists did not think of a handicapped person as one of themselves. Part of Sean O'Casey's autobiography concerns the famous meeting when Larkin appears at a window of the Imperial Hotel. O'Casey says that it was time for the crippled and maimed to get off the street so that the working man can fight for his rights. The famous playwright is expressing the general attitude of his time: that anyone permanently in a wheelchair or with any other serious disability is beyond wanting to fight for his rights or, worse still, incapable of identifying with his fellow man.

Nothing really changed untillthe 1960s and '70s when Liam Maguire became active in the trade union movement. As TD Pat Rabbitte says: "The whole business of the disabled in Ireland is a subculture which doesn't really touch on the rest of society that much." Pat Rabbitte says the "modest" appreciation he now has of people with disabilities is largely due to Liam Maguire. "Because it was he who, as he would put it himself, "straightened out my views on the disabled and the handicapped. In the sense," Pat continues, "that he felt a lot of leftwing people had views on the disabled which were very woolly and hazy, and he hated do-gooders for do-gooders' sake." For Pat Rabbitte Liam was an ambassador for the disabled community in the broader labour movement. "He was, probably for most of us, the only personality of any strength and significance that we knew amongst the disabled."

The 1978 Annual Delegate Conference of the Irish Congress of Trade Unions plays a pivotal role in Maguire's trade union career. It was at that conference that Liam moved Resolution 60 on the Rights of Disabled Persons. The speech supporting this motion is very powerful indeed. Even reading it in cold print, one can hear a voice echo around the room. For those who knew him, it is Liam Maguire's voice, but equally it could be Keir Hardie's or Martin Luther King's :

Mindful of the United Nations General Assembly Resolution 3447 "Declaration on the Rights of Disabled Persons" adopted on 9th December 1975 and being aware of the contents of the paper "A Fair Deal for the Handicapped" delivered by the Chairman of the Irish Wheelchair Association to the Union of Voluntary Organisations for the Handicapped on 15th October 1977, this Conference instructs the General Executive Committee of Congress to:

1. Re-title the Sub Committee on Protective Legislation to include "and Legislation for the Handicapped" and to expand its membership.
2. Make immediate and strong representation to the Government to:
    Declare a date by which all existing buildings and services occupied by Government Department, Local Authority and other State Bodies shall be made fully accessible to the physically handicapped.
    Ensure that the already overdue National Building Code will have adequate provisions for accessibility for

the physically handicapped and punitive penalties for failure to observe same.

Establish, in conjunction with Diploma- and Degree -awarding bodies, a method whereby the curricula and examinations for architects and civil engineers shall include accessibility for the physically handicapped.

Declare the principle that public transportation must be made accessible to the physically handicapped and to give a commitment that future capital expenditure will include provision for such accessibility.

Ensure that all schools, colleges, and universities are made fully accessible to the physically handicapped and to give a commitment that future capital expenditure from State funds will be given only where there is provision for such accessibility.

Establish that in each Planning Office there is one named individual with specific responsibility and training for ensuring that accessibility requirements are met.

Recognise that a handicapped worker without a job is unemployed rather than ill by transferring the responsibility for training and placement of the handicapped to the Minister for Labour.

Publish the entire Resolution and Declaration on the Rights of Disabled Persons in the national newspapers in order to comply with article 13 of the Resolution.

3. Enter into discussions with the Government and the Employer-Labour Conference with a view to establishing a regular comprehensive medical check-up for every worker in the country to prevent or to detect at an early stage, any serious illness or defect.

4. Make representations to the Taoiseach to appoint a Minister of State for the Handicapped with specific responsibilities to include liaison with ICTU and the national voluntary organisations catering for the handicapped.

5. Include a section in next year's report to advise Conference of progress on this Resolution.

Maguire continued:

In proposing this motion from my Union it is first of all necessary to state that we accept the amendment proposed by the Federation of Rural Workers. We do not wish to have the motion become contentious by insisting on the inclusion of a part which might cause difficulty within the Executive Council of Congress. However we believe that a few words of explanation of the need for the amendment would assist clarification for the record, if the mover of the amendment would so oblige. It is not my intention to speak at any great length about the contents of the motion, for two reasons. One, each delegate here has received a copy of the documents referred to in the first paragraph. In the Wexford speech there is amplification of each of the points referred to, so I will not take up time by repeating them. Secondly, the speech was circulated to the Executive Council of each of the unions and trade councils within the Republic of Ireland—which Government is being called upon to act—and a large number of them responded. Therefore I would like to have the maximum amount of time to speak here today for the record.

I wish now to express my thanks to those trade unions and trade councils who considered the points raised in the speech and who made representations to the various Ministers and relevant Departments.

While there is no doubt in my mind that this motion will be adopted by Congress, I must emphasise the importance of continuing consciousness of the matter. There is no one here today who is unaffected by the reality of handicap in our community whether you are handicapped yourself, or have parents or children or relatives or friends who are handicapped. For too long it has been left to voluntary organisations, with little or no State assistance, to attempt to cope with all the needs of the handicapped. Voluntary organisations are not the answer. State consciousness and State commitment are the answer. Each time we establish a new, voluntary organisation for a new minority group who are handi-capped, we further perpetuate the inequality and divi-siveness. On the day that we identify handicap in a child, and then cope with that handicap by organising a sepa-rate environment for that child, that is the day we lay the foundations for the massive wall that will forever sepa-rate that child from his peers. When he or she grows into adulthood it will have been a very real apartheid—

separate development—that will have occurred.

We rightly condemn the system of apartheid in South Africa as being inhuman and an affront to the dignity of man. Is it so vastly different for those handicapped in Ireland who cannot use public transport, public buildings, educational facilities, and social facilities? How dignified is it for me to be carried up the stairs to this Conference? The willingness of people to help is not in question—it never has been. What is in question is the affront to my dignity and my person every time I am confronted with an obstacle that bars me from circulating freely in my own society. There is no escape from these affronts and there will be none until positive moves are made to eliminate them.

Be under no misapprehension. We are not talking solely about the 4,000 wheelchair users in our society today, although if we were it would make the case no less valid. The worker who has a disabling accident tomorrow is, from that moment, in a different world. It does not matter who or what he is today, tomorrow the apartheid begins to work against him.

It is not my intention to dwell exclusively on the question of accessibility. There is another extremely important point contained in paragraph 3 of the motion, a point of great importance to all working people and their families. I will quote directly from the Wexford speech:

"...Many disabilities can be avoided through preventive medicine. It is our firm belief that all of our people should have regular medical checks and the onus is on the State to provide this service. This is particularly important for school children and industrial workers, for whom these checks should be at least annual and as mandatory as is constitutionally possible..."

The switch in emphasis from curative to preventive medicine is a dramatic one which will require great political will and determination to ensure that the interests of all the people are not sacrificed to the self-interest of the few.

If we want to build a better society, and equal society for our handicapped, then we must start now. Each one of us in our own way can be constructive by considering the problems of the handicapped and by using our voices and our votes. Nothing so moves a politician as a vote in jeopardy! It is the politicians we must move - they must legislate and implement that legislation.

I urge this delegate conference of the Irish Congress of Trade Unions to show the Irish people and the Government and those international agencies of rehabilitation, which will be informed about the outcome of this Conference decision, of the determination of the organised working class in this country to propagate and defend the rights of the handicapped and to pursue the issues raised in the motion.

Resolution 60 was formally seconded by Denis Larkin, a direct descendant of the great Jim Larkin. Mr Larkin said: "In seconding this motion I want to bring sharply to the attention of Congress that we are concerned with the right of the handicapped to be put in a position to play their full role as people in the work force and to make a full contribution to the progress of the community." After making the point that those who have been engaged in working for the handicapped in voluntary organisations deserve praise, Larkin says; "However, as the mover of the motion said, we must move forward. It is not just a question of voluntary support, the handicapped need to be put in the position as a result of legislation and Government and community action so that they can play a full role in the affairs of their community."

Two other handicapped people also contributed to the debate. Micheal O'Reagan of the Bakery and Food Workers' Amalgamated Union criticised the government for not providing adequate funds for the training of guide dogs for the blind. Des Kenny, representing the National League of the Blind of Ireland, said:

In commending this motion to delegates one should point out something which is a growing phemonenon within the trade union movement, and which we hope will become part of its general demeanour, and that is the fact that the motion was proposed by someone like Liam Maguire; delegates have heard Micheal O'Reagan speak to it and now you hear me speak to the motion. Up to some years ago you would expect to see us three in Lourdes rather than at a conference like this and it is an important aspect of the rehabilitation of the disabled, an aspect which is resented by rehabilitors to some extent, that we are expressing and articulating the needs of people who are perhaps less articulate than us but who are handicapped as we are.

The motion was carried without controversy.

In replying to the debate Liam thanked the contributers and assured Senator Jack Harte that the handicapped people would welcome a motion being put down in the Seanad where a minister would have to respond. "I believe that what is happening here today is unique in international trade unionism."

A lot of handicapped people would say; "So what!" Several times Liam's close friend, Harry Ellis, has expressed disappointment at the lack of effective action on the part of the unions on issues concerning the disabled. During an interview in 1985 Colm O'Doherty, active in the Irish Wheelchair Association since 1980, complains of the trade unions at Dublin Airport being unable to decide who should operate a vehicle designed to transport disabled passengers from the terminal to their plane. It has also been said that Liam wanted a strike at the factory if new buses for public transport were not made accessible to wheelchair users, but he did not get the support of the trade unions involved.

While I was researching a newspaper article in 1981 I put similar points to Maguire. He argued that making the statement and having it unanimously accepted by Congress was just a first step. A copy of Liam's speech, "A Fair Deal for the Handicapped", delivered in 1977, was sent to the executive of every trade union as well as every TD and Senator. Early in 1978 the ICTU executive endorsed United Nations Resolution 3447 on the rights of the handicapped. Resolution 60 made direct reference to Resolution 3447 and "A Fair Deal for the Handicapped". "About the same time," Maguire said, "the trade union representatives on the National Economic and Social Council looked for, and eventually got, a report on the status and position of disabled people in Ireland. The NESC issued its report on Services for Mentally and Physically Handicapped Persons in 1980, and the National Understanding made a demand for the Government to issue a Green Paper on the rights of disabled people." Maguire stated that these two things did not happen by accident. "There was a pattern to all of this," he said. "If the government doesn't produce the Green Paper we have the trade union movement to jump up-and-down on them on our behalf."

Peter Cassells of the Irish Congress of Trade Unions talked to us about the initiatives that flowed from Resolution 60. A major seminar took place on 19 May 1979 at which officials from various unions heard contributions from people like Pauline Faughnan of The Irish Wheelchair Association, who spoke of the lack of statistical information on the "needs or even numbers and extent of disability" in Ireland. Frank Flannery, General Manager of the Rehabilitation Institute, delivered a paper on the Economics of Rehabilition, and outlined a survey which found that for every £1 the economy spent on rehabilitation the return was £24. While advising caution Flannery concluded: "sufficient evidence emerges to show that the high return on investment in rehabilitation in human and social terms is complemented by a handsome return to the economy in increased national income." Dr J A Robins, from the Department of Health, spoke on "Training and Employing the Handicapped."

In initiating these seminars and pushing the cause of the disabled through various National Understandings Liam was slowly influencing trade unionists in order that they might bring pressure to bear on the legislators. He also spread the gospel by attending conferences of unions other than his own. John Hall said that Liam attended a conference of the Association of Scientific, Technical and Managerial Staffs as their only ever guest speaker where he "went down a storm." But was this enough?

In 1981 Liam said it was a little naive to think a national strike would take place on behalf of the disabled. "The real strength," he argued, "is in centralised bargaining; the elements of a National Understanding referring to the disabled will have to be reported on each year and there will have to be improvements each time. The advantage is if the disabled make certain demands and get no satisfaction we can simply get the trade unions movement, the big brothers, to get in there and make the same demands and the government can't ignore them the way it can ignore us."

However, Des Kenny has not got the same faith in "Big Brother." He says Congress put a demand for all state-sponsored bodies to employ a three percent quota of disabled people into the 1980 National Understanding but has done nothing to see that it is fulfilled. He also points out that since 1968 the National League of the Blind have got the ICTU to pass resolutions that the pension for the blind should not be means-tested, but the situation has not changed regarding this pension. "They write it down on a piece of paper and send it to the minister, but they don't fight cver it."

This author spoke to Don Murphy of the Civil Service Executive Union on the subject of the proposed three percent quota of public sector jobs being reserved for disabled people. He claimed his union were "strong movers" in supporting this measure, but that the cutbacks in job opportunities in the civil service generally are having a disproportionate effect on disabled people.

Despite his criticisms Des Kenny does value the commitment of trade union activists to the rights of the disabled, but fears what may become of that commitment without someone like Maguire to keep pushing. He says: "It's only as disabled people are interested in other people that other people will become interested in their problems." Des Kenny feels that the concern Liam Maguire showed for trade unions generally was reciprocated and came his way when he needed it.

To the suggestion that trade unions just pass resolutions supporting the disabled and nothing else, Colm O'Doherty seems to accept the value of having an article such as Resolution 60 set down on record, but says the trade unions have not fulfilled their commitment in their own sphere of influence.

On the other hand, Pauline Faughnan points out that almost all the impetus for a National Economic and Social Council report on the handicapped came from the trade union influence on the NESC committee. The NESC report was well received when it was published in 1980, and accepted as the basis for a Government Green Paper. Faughnan says she was told by a top civil servant: "You have written the Green Paper for us."

Chapter 12

In the late 1970s, following the publication of Pauline Faughnan's *The Dimensions of Need*, the Irish Wheelchair Association published a number of policy documents. According to the Association's Chief Executive Officer, Phil O'Meachair, the document on accessibility and mobility was almost exclusively the work of Liam Maguire. On public transport the document states: "an appropriate public transport service—increasingly recognised and accepted as a social amenity—must cater for all who wish to avail of such a service. Existing provisions virtually exclude the wheelchair user." Maguire's demands included: "All railway stations must be accessible to and usable by a person in a wheelchair or by any person with impaired mobility." He wanted at least one coach on each train to be accessible, "with an accessible toilet incorporated or adjacent thereto," and new rolling stock "should incorporate provision, at the design stage, for use by a person in a wheelchair."

On buses and subways Maguire wrote: "Existing technology should be utilised to make buses accessible, as is the position in Seattle, Washington and Berkeley, California, to name but two, and on subway systems of Washington DC and San Francisco."

As early as May 1977, representatives of the National Rehabilitation Board's Access for The

Disabled Committee met with representatives from CIE. Like all such first meetings it seems to have had the atmosphere of the two sides sizing each other up. On the subject of buses Mr Healy of CIE said that a hoist would present major problems as a result of the light structure of the buses, but a ramp might be considered.

In September Liam reported that he had received information from three American bus manufacturers to the effect that all buses to be built by them after 30 September 1979 must be accessible to the handicapped. His files contain a letter dated 6 July from a George Prytula of ROHR Industries in Washington DC Referring to the "kneeling" capabilities of his company's buses Mr Prytula wrote: "Since the process is so simple, we do not have much literature to cover it. The cost for the modification is a relatively few hundred dollars per bus."

George Prytula did enclose photographs and written descriptions of the kneeling bus. The kneeling bus has "air suspension" which, I remember Liam telling me, is the same as that fitted in Citroën cars. To allow a wheelchair to enter the driver can very easily deflate the suspension to lower the floor at the entrance. In conjunction with the kneeling front suspension, the entrance steps are hydraulically extended into a platform lift "with overall dimensions of approximately 34 inches square, plus a 29 inches by 14 inches access ramp."

Also described is a wheelchair restraint system incorporating a three-passenger folding seat for use when no wheelchair user is on the bus. Liam also received information on kneeling buses from General Motors and AM General Corporation in Michigan.

The author has access to the details of two

further meetings the NRB commitee had with CIE, but the only positive indication on access to buses— which was Maguire's immediate concern as a new bus fleet was about to be built—is that on 26 April 1978, CIE agreed to consider reserving seats near the entrance for elderly and handicapped passengers.

Although Liam was down to attend all these meetings, as a NRB committee member, in fact he attended none. Apparently, true to his style, he preferred to run the campaign single-handedly through the trade union movement. He used his capacity as IWA chairman, and later as chairman of the Association's 1981 International Year of the Disabled Persons committee. Between 1979 and 1981 he corresponded with, among other trade unionists and politicians, Peter Cassells, Paddy Brogan (both of the ICTU) and Liam St John Devlin, then chairman of CIE.

In an interview with this author Liam St John Devlin said of one visit to the United States: "I did the round of the authorities in the States who were providing special facilities for handicapped." The former CIE chairman says he visited Washington DC, New York and Seattle and also spoke to those responsible in Toronto. He talked about the use of public transport by disabled people being under 0.1%, and in Washington DC the lifts were not properly maintained because of this lack of use.

In reply to this, no doubt, Maguire would point to a report produced by Synergy Consulting Services, for and by the disabled, in California dated July 1980. The Synergy report argues that the American Public Transit Association deliberately misrepresents the situation by calculating the percentage of disabled passengers to the entire numbers using systems which are not "anything like 50% accessibility, let alone 100% accessibility." Synergy makes the point that unless all the buses on a line are completely accessible, and disabled people can exchange from one line to another as easily as an able-bodied person, then the number of disabled passengers cannot be compared with the overall usage.

Hugh Geraghty of the Amalgamated Union of Engineering Workers sees it in the context of the CIE Group of Unions trying to persuade management that the company should build its own buses instead of giving the contract to an outside company. He writes: "When Liam attended the group meeting on 6 February 1980, he showed us pictures of buses which were in use in Europe and the USA. He advised us that he had made various approaches by way of letters and seeking to meet CIE management people to discuss the possibility of using a design suitable for the disabled. He even pointed out that London buses and buses elsewhere in Britain at least had the facility of being able to take on a wheelchair and lock it in position. In their anxiety to win the battle with the group of unions, the Company were not prepared to consider what Liam had to say. It was at that stage he came to seek our assistance."

Geraghty says that Liam joined the group for their next meeting with management where they raised the issue of design. Up until then the unions' only concern was that the building of the buses should be done by CIE itself, and meanwhile management forged ahead developing the design they wanted. Hugh Geraghty says management was determined to go ahead without any interference from Liam or anyone else: "in order that the policy that they had embarked upon would be carried through." He says the features Liam wanted would have been just marginally more expensive if planned for at the design stage, but the impression he got was that CIE management wanted to keep out of Liam's way as much as possible.

From 1979 through 1980 and into 1981 Paddy Brogan, CIE Trade Union Group Secretary, and Liam as well, were writing to CIE's chairman and to various politicians on the issue of accessibility to buses. The response from virtually all the politicians was the standard one in such situations, expressing support without giving any commitment.

Some TDs did write to Mr Devlin, but to each one the CIE chairman replied: "Life is very difficult for CIE, one is continually abused about the size of the deficit, one is continually trying to cut costs and reduce manpower. At the same time one is continually under pressure to extend social services. No government has recognised the social aspect of transport, all are only concerned with the deficit."

Paddy Brogan expressed some sympathy for the company. Even in 1977 plans for the Bombardier bus were so far advanced that it would have been very difficult to make modifications because there was an assembly-line approach. He says that if CIE had been building the buses themselves at their old workshops in Inchicore, Dublin, where there is a tradition of skilled coach-building, there might have been some hope. "Although," says Brogan, "I wouldn't in any way discourage Liam, because he had achieved so much, anything was conceivable."

It must be said that Mr St John Devlin's respect for Liam came through very obviously in his interview with this writer. With some sadness he recalls Maguire saying openly such things as: "Liam

Devlin is not a good man." It is a sign of the working friendship the two had that Liam told him about his motorcycle accident. However, Maguire, the socialist, would have disapproved of CIE handing over their bus-building operation to private enterprise. In this he would have great empathy with the shopworkers' struggle to keep bus- and coach-building in Inchicore.

On 22 May 1980 Deputy John O'Connell and three other Labour MEPs tabled "A Charter of Rights for the Disabled" in the European Parliament, which included a call for access to public transport. However, in a Department of Health survey—sent to the then Taoiseach, Jack Lynch, on 20 November 1979—it is reported: "CIE state that, since early 1977, they have had a series of discussions with the National Rehabilitation Board. CIE maintain that the NRB accepts (though certain bodies it represents do not) that it would not be possible to alter existing arrangements in public transport so as to significantly improve access by handicapped and disabled people."

It is important here to remember that Liam had been on the NRB's board of directors since 1977. As with other aspects of this biography, the author's intention was to treat this subject as objectively as possible. However, when the NRB's Medical Director, Thomas M. Gregg, was contacted he saw fit not to give information on this. The main paragraph of Dr Gregg's letter to the author, dated 1 March 1985, reads: "I feel sure you will appreciate that the discussion with the NRB and CIE is private to the committee that is responsible for same."

In an address to the Union of Students in Ireland on 17 January 1981 Liam stated:

The matter of mobility-impairment is a matter which affects huge numbers of our population. Our people cannot be said to be exercising their right to fully participate in the life of the community if they are confined to their own homes or institutions and to an area within a radius of a couple of hundred yards of those domiciles. We are not here referring to merely the 5,000 or so people in wheelchairs. We have 350,000 people over 65 years of age and it is estimated that at least one-third of these have severe mobility impairment. In addition there are, at any one time, some 100,000 people on long-term disability benefit due to permanent or long-term handicap. Great numbers of these people suffer from mobility-impairment. An accessible public transport system would enable many of these people to circulate in the community. Many cities in other countries have such systems. The Irish Congress of Trade Unions recognised the need for an accessible public transport system when its Annual Delegate Conference in 1978 unanimously supported the reasonable demand that future capital expenditure must contain provision for such accessibility. Subsequent to that being adopted a decision was taken by C.I.E management to commission a Canadian bus-building company, Bombardier, in Shannon to build a new national fleet of some 750 buses. The technology is available to make those buses wheelchair- accessible and, indeed, pram accessible! However, despite representations from the Irish Wheelchair Association, the CIE Shopworkers' Group, Limerick Trades Council, the Executive Committee of Congress, the National Rehabilitation Board, and deputies and Senators from all parties, the Chairman and management of CIE have failed to discuss the matter in a positive and helpful manner.

Maguire makes reference to the then European Transport Commissioner, Richard Burke, who wrote to Vice-President Vredeling: "The Technology is available to make buses and trains accessible to wheelchairs. We should investigate the possibilities of having mandatory access to all means of transport." Vice-President Vredeling replied in part: "that the Community must facilitate the utilisation of means of transport by handicapped persons and that Directorate-General V and Directorate-General VII should collaborate in the preparation of initiatives to be undertaken."

Maguire continued from there: "Won't it be ironic if, once again, 'a social order in which justice and charity shall inform all the institutions of the national life' (quoting the Irish constitution) will be forced on us, not by our own actions, but by the European Community?"

Finally: "Also, apart from the social desirability of helping mobility impaired people to get about, think of the possible job-creation potential if we were the European suppliers of wheelchair-accessible public buses, as certainly, buses will have to be some day, because disabled people are becoming more organised and more aware of their legal and civil rights."

In March 1981 Liam wrote: "The state-of-the-art in accessible public transport is most advanced in the United States. This is largely because section 504 of the 1973 Rehabilitation Act precludes the granting of federal funds to any organisation that discriminates on the basis of handicap." The letter points out that "Seattle Metro is running 143 accessible buses out of a fleet of 900. After only a few months seventy people a day are riding those buses. The lifts cost $5,700 and have proven 98% reliable.

"AC Transit, like Seattle Metro, is truly trying to make accessibility work. AC will reach program accessibility by July 1982, and the cost for the lifts will be $4,800,000. This will be a fifteen-year investment, the lifetime of AC Transit's buses. Contrast this with the costs of special paratransit services now provided in Alameda and Contra Costa counties through state transit funds. For fiscal year 1980-81 the two counties' paratransit services within AC's operating district will amount to a total of $2,030,950!! Paratransit, (separate specialised transport for disabled people)" says Maguire, "is not cheap."

Maguire documents how "some elements within APTA [Association of Public Transit Authorities] have propagandised and misinformed the public about the costs of accessible buses and have propagated the myth that specialised services are the solution to the problem of mobility for handicapped people..."

"Finally," Maguire writes, "the United States' Department of Transportation, in its own official report, *Comments on Transportation for Handicapped Persons*, states, in part, "...Moreover it is much less expensive and more cost effective to make existing transportation systems accessible to handicapped persons than it is to create separate, special systems just to serve a small numbers of handicapped individuals with very limited transportation options. This is particularly true for fixed route bus systems where the Department's section 504 regulation simply requires that when new buses are purchased for normal replacement purposes, those buses will include lifts to assist handicapped persons in boarding. (Such lifts cost approximately $10,000 in new buses, of which the local cost share is 20%, or approximately $2,000.)

"Whereas the lifts, once purchased, can be used for the 12-to-15 year life of the buses, special systems have continuing high operating costs in addition to their initial capital costs. For example the deficit for the City of Omaha's special services for handicapped persons is approximately $454,000 annually—11% of the City's UMTA Section 5 grant funds. Moreover, these special systems typically do not provide service comparable to the main transit service, in that they have numerous restrictions in terms of hours of operation, geographic scope, waiting costs, trip purposes, advance reservation times etc."

Maguire himself argued that the costs of operating a parallel system would become greater as time goes on. "An accessible public transport system would undoubtedly reduce the considerable cost of providing specialised services."

The authorities remained unconvinced. On 14 April Peter Cassells of the Irish Congress of Trade Unions wrote to Mr St John Devlin suggesting "that a team from CIE should visit those American cities which have undertaken or are currently planning a programme for accessible public transport. Such a team should consist of the Chief Executive, an engineer, a workers' representative and a representative from the Irish Wheelchair Association."

It would have been interesting if Maguire had joined such a group, but obviously Mr Devlin did not consider it a serious proposition. "I had enough problems at that stage," he told this author. Maria Cassidy talks about Liam fighting with the NRB board, who, it seems, actually supported CIE on this issue. She says at this stage he felt very much alone, and even disabled people themselves seemed unwilling to be angry.

In May 1981 CIE launched one specialist single-deck bus. The CIE chairman intended a pilot project whereby disabled people could phone for the bus some days in advance, and CIE would also pick up disabled people in a certain area to bring them

to work each morning and leave them home at the
end of the day. Liam Maguire and the IWA
dismissed this as totally inadequate, and the idea
was never put into operation.

Chapter 13

Liam wanted new legislation to underpin the rights of disabled people. The achievement of rights, not charity, for disabled people was the driving force in his life. In 1981 when asked about pressure groups of disabled people in other countries, he told the author that disabled people are best organised in the United States and the Scandinavian countries simply because they have the laws. "Statutory legislation, underwriting their position. There are," he went on, "finances available from Federal funding to enable disabled organisations to organize themselves."

One could not talk long in this vein with Liam before he mentioned the United States 1973 Rehabilitation Act. Section 504 of this act reads: "No otherwise qualified handicapped individual in the United States, as defined in Section 7 (6), shall solely by reason of his handicap be excluded from the participation in, be denied the benefits of, or be subjected to discrimination under any programme or activity receiving federal finance assistance." Liam Maguire wanted similar laws in Ireland.

But he was not going to wait around for things to happen. Given the slightest opportunity he was off on a one-man crusade. On 1 February 1979 there came in the post a summons to attend jury duty at the Four Courts, Dublin in the name of John

(Liam's proper first name) William Maguire. Liam filled in the requisite documentation and enclosed a letter, the key paragraph of which stated:

> You are probably unaware that I am paraplegic, and consequently must use a wheelchair for mobility. You will understand that architectural barriers are a source of frustration and indignity to me and to all wheelchair users. Prior to my appearance on the date appointed I would be most grateful to hear from you that no such architectural barriers will impede me from performing my jury duty.

At this stage we can only speculate. Did he know what was coming? Had he a master plan already hatched in his mind? Probably he had an idea of what would happen next.

On 12 February 1979 the County Registrar wrote to Liam:

> Since the Courtrooms in the Four Courts contain a large amount of steps and the jury rooms off the courts are upstairs, it would be very difficult for you to perform jury service. As these types of barriers are a source of frustration and indignity to you I am removing your name from the panel of Jurors for these present sittings. Accordingly your attendance in Court on foot of the summons served will not be necessary.

One almost feels sympathy for officialdom. Ah, come on Liam, they *are* being considerate. But you cannot give a dog a bone and expect to take it back with a pat on his head. The dog bites.

> Thank you for your letter of 12th February and also for form J8 received today. You will recollect the opening sentence of my letter of 1st February which read as follows: 'Please find enclosed form J2 received this morning. I have signed the document having made the declaration I have read Note 12 and I am qualified for

jury service.' I have not asked to be excused as a right nor at the discretion of the County Registrar. I would be most grateful, therefore, if you would be so kind as to inform me under which provision of the Juries or other Act I have been removed from the panel of Jurors for these present sittings.

The postal strike of 1979 intervened and on 15 July Liam rewrote the same letter to the County Registrar.

The remaining days of July passed by and August was coming to a close. On 29 August Liam wrote again to the County Registrar reminding him that he had not replied to his letters of 16 February and 15 July.

On 5 September the County Registrar wrote to Liam:

I acknowledge receipt of your letter dated 29th August 1979. As a result of the information contained in your original letter dated 1st February 1979, and for reasons outlined in my reply dated February 12th—copy herewith—you are excused from attending. Jurors may be excused from jury service under Section 9 of the 1976 Act.

For the fainthearted—such as this writer—this probably would have been the end. But the chessplayer in Liam Maguire had just completed his opening moves. We are now into the middle game.

Senator Mary Robinson talked about Liam's attitude to the law as being very confident. "A lot of people," she says, "particularly those who come to a barrister, are very often intimidated or even cowed. But when I would meet Liam, perhaps in the Four Courts I would have my wig and gown on, or meeting him in my chambers dressed like this (ordinary clothes), it didn't really matter where we met, it was always on completely equal and completely relaxed terms."

For the remaining months of 1979 and through 1980 Liam was in contact with Mary Robinson and solicitor Sean Sexton. Despite this, nothing appears to have happened. Pat McCartan seems anxious to point out that on this case Liam parted with Sean Sexton on the most amicable terms and this is borne out when Sexton says he subsequently did work of a personal nature for Liam. Sean Sexton explained that his practice is not geared for constitutional cases and Liam said he had someone else willing to take on his case.

Liam met solicitor Pat McCartan in the Royal Dublin Hotel in O'Connell Street on 3 April 1981. They met there because Pat's offices were inaccessible to wheelchairs. They had a brief talk in which Liam outlined his story and Pat agreed to take up the case as long as Sean Sexton was agreeable to hand over to him.

It was a meeting of like minds. McCartan himself had been a member of the Workers' Party since his student days in the early 1970s. He talks about being one of those who had no contact with disabled people and he did not realise their capabilities. "The first thing I noticed was that Liam crossed O'Connell Street in peak traffic in his wheelchair to get to me on his own, and then mounted the footpath and came in the front door—*that in itself*."

If McCartan had the traditional "hopeless helpless cripple" view of disabled people, Maguire was not too long in educating him. Pat took on the issue as if it was his own, and it's easy to see that he fully understood the importance of disabled people being allowed to play a full role in society.

The next step for Pat McCartan was to inform

Senator Robinson that he was now solicitor for Liam. He also asked Ercus Stewart, then a junior counsel, to start drafting proceedings.

On 6 May 1981 McCartan wrote to the County Registrar with the information that he was acting for the plaintiff and had consulted counsel. The letter reiterates Liam's determination to be considered eligible for jury duty and invites the Registrar to meet with Liam to discuss his position and decide what steps might be taken to facilitate him.

One of the reasons for suggesting such a meeting, Pat McCartan says, "was that they would see that Liam was not a crank—see that he was someone who was articulate and intelligent and well capable of carrying out the functions of being a juror. And also to see that he was a very persistent man." The second reason for the proposed meeting, Pat tells us, was so that Liam could put any points he felt could be put to facilitate his acting as a juror.

"Did they meet?"

"No, they did not," McCartan says emphatically. While pointing out the impossibility of knowing specifically what was in the authorities' minds, he says that they quite clearly decided to keep Liam at a distance and deal with the case through the lawyers on a completely impersonal basis. "It was obviously felt," McCartan continues, "that if they were to meet Liam directly, they might well compromise themselves in whatever position they had decided to take—they might make admissions to him, they might let slip something that would be of detriment to them at the eventual hearing. They were beginning to respect him, in other words."

The letter of 6 May 1981 outlines Liam's active participation in organisations such as the Irish Wheelchair Association, the National Rehabilitation Board, The Federated Workers' Union of Ireland and the Presidium d'Action Européenne des Handicappés. The latter is an organisation within the European Parliament. "That kind of thing," McCartan says, "must have really scared them because they realised they had a man who wasn't simply paraplegic—there was an awful lot more to him'.

On 9 May Ercus Stewart wrote to McCartan asking him to obtain from Liam information on the facilities for disabled people in courts in other countries. The case was being made. Pat McCartan says the idea was to show that in other jurisdictions of a similar type of law to Ireland such as the Common Law of Canada, the US, England and Sweden, disabled people were facilitated and that it could be done.

Liam got information on two specific situations. In California, the Department of Rehabilitation brought a court action against the County of Napa to prevent the use of Federal Funds for the renovation of the County courtroom. The walkway to the courthouse, the witness stand, the judge's bench, court clerk's desk, judge's chambers and adjacent restrooms were all inaccessible to wheelchair users.

Newspaper reports for October-November 1980 state that the Treasury Department's office of the Revenue Sharing ordered Napa to construct ramps to jury boxes, witness stands, clerk's desks etc. It was advised that the demand for a ramp to the judges' benches be dropped because the then present judges wrote that steps accommodated their respective handicaps better. At the same time it was ruled that permanent ramps be installed when either or both judges left their post.

Sacramento County saw the first deaf person to act as a juror in 1980. There was an intrepreter of sign language in court to help with communications and, far from feeling that there were any problems involved, the other jurors elected the deaf person as foreman.

Curtis Brewer, who is completely paralysed from the neck down, is a lawyer with his practice in New York. *Disabled USA* magazine quotes Brewer as saying "The question is, what do we really want in terms of being disabled? Do we want our rights vigorously, or passively expect to have them given to us? If it is the latter, then we are guilty of masochistically compounding the patronization we experience."

Whatever else they might justifiably accuse him of, nobody can ever say that Liam Maguire passively waited for his rights to be handed to him. But he had a mountain to climb, and in 1981 that mountain in Ireland was several times higher than in the United States. There he would have had the 1973 Rehabilitation Act as a relatively secure platform.

The question to be answered was, did Liam have the right to act as a juror in the eyes of Irish law. In order to explore this, Liam's lawyers invited us to examine three previous judgments made in Irish courts.

In a letter dated 1 July Ercus Stewart refers to the case of de Burca versus the State. In 1975 Máirín de Burca and Mary Anderson successfully challenged the constitutionality of the 1927 Juries Act because it included just ratepayers and women had to apply to be considered. Ercus Stewart quotes three times the de Burca/Anderson case.

Firstly Mr Justice Walsh states:

I am satisfied that the constitutional provision relating to trial with a jury, or the other provisions of the constitution relied upon which I deal with in greater detail, do not prevent the Oireachtas from validly enacting that certain categories of the citizens or inhabitants of the State by virtue of their *physical* (Stewart's emphasis) or moral capacity could properly be excluded from either the obligation or qualification to serve as jurors.

Justice Walsh later states:

From one viewpoint, jury service may be regarded as a privilege, but from another, exemption from jury service may be regarded as a privilege - just as liberty to avoid any obligation or duty which falls on other people may be regarded as a privilege. The question is whether the "privilege" is of a type that can be validly conferred by statute.

Ercus Stewart also quotes Mr. Justice Griffin on the same case:

It seems to me that there can no longer be (if there ever was) any justification for exempting women from the duty or *privilege* of jury service.

Again the emphasis is Ercus Stewart's. "Unfortunately," he concludes, "nowhere is the right to serve on a jury referred to as a right, it is referred to as a duty, privilege, liability, obligation, etc."

Did Liam Maguire in the eyes of the Irish law have the right to serve on a jury and was the exclusion because of his disability an invidious discrimination? A lay person, especially if that person is disabled, might say it is invidious and offensive to declare that because of his inability to walk he was deemed unfit to perform a useful function in society.

However, in the de Burca case, the plaintiffs had

137

originally been on a criminal charge, and when they came before a jury trial they claimed that because under the 1927 Act the obligation of jury service was restricted to a small number of propertied males, this could lead to an inbuilt, if unconscious, bias on their part in a particular trial. Thus in his letter of 1 June, Ercus Stewart suggests if Liam knew of a disabled person involved in criminal proceedings wishing to object to trial by reason of unfair selection of jury, this person might be a very useful plaintiff.

Also in the de Burca trial, Justice O'Higgins refers to the United States Supreme Court decision in *Hoyt versus Florida*, which declared that under a statute similar to the 1927 Act, so long as a woman could apply to serve if she wished, there was no arbitrary exclusion of women from jury service. When asked whether it could be argued that there was an arbitrary decision to exclude Liam Maguire because he was a paraplegic, Senator Mary Robinson says :

> There were a number of different approaches which we adopted in the statement of claim, and that certainly would have been part of the argument to be made.
>
> The de Burca judgment was one we would have relied upon in a number of ways, but it also had the kind of difficulties in that a number of judges did not conclude on whether it was a right [jury service] or a duty. But I think what they said was whether it's a right or whether it's a responsibility of citizenship, citizens have a right to be equally considered in relation to it or have a right to a random selection.

"One of the arguments we had to make on behalf of Liam," says Pat McCartan, "was that he had in fact a concomitant right to act as a juror given that he had been called to do so, and that he couldn't simply just be dropped at the whim of the common good or the mere convenience of the common good, as expressed by the Registrar of the court."

Still on the question of whether someone like Liam, or indeed anyone, has the right to be a juror, Pat McCartan says "...that is something that is hazy and there are a lot of references to it in the de Burca case. They are saying that it is perhaps not so, but it was essential to our case with Liam."

The de Burca case which led to the 1976 Juries Act is, according to McCartan "a hallmark judgment dealing with the whole question of what can amount to discrimination—and particularly the words invidious discrimination are important."

Pat McCartan says that when Eamon de Valera wrote the Irish constitution in 1937, "everything he gave by rights with one hand under Articles 40-44 he took away with the other hand. He has these saving clauses that there shouldn't be discrimination or invidious discrimination on physical or moral grounds save what is in the common good. This is an area we were afraid we were going to fall into."

Pat McCartan then refers to David Norris who brought his action claiming that criminal legislation against homosexual men was wrong. Norris lost his case because of this "save what is in the common good" clause.

When we examine the judgment in the David Norris case it is easy to see what Pat McCartan means. To this writer, for whom researching this chapter was the first serious study of any legal matters, it seems that the grounds for the rejection of Norris's claim do not have the sort of objectivity one might expect.

The reasons given for the decision can be

summarised thus: homosexual acts between consenting adults have always been looked upon as wrong and repugnant in the eyes of public opinion. We must remember here that the Norris case was in the early 1980s before the issue of AIDS was uppermost in the public mind. Reading through the David Norris case, this writer wonders whether such equally subjective reasoning could be given for the dismissal of Liam's claim, such as that the majority of people expect those in wheelchairs, or with any other serious disability, to play a passive role in society, or even that some disabled people with a less positive self-image might feel incapable of doing jury service.

Before we continue, it is neccessary to explain a few technicalities. After the approach is made by the client through his solicitor, the junior counsel sets about preparing the draft pleadings. It was in this context that Ercus Stewart put the questions contained in his letters of 9 May and 1 June. When junior counsel has done this the senior counsel looks over them, saying what to leave in and what to take out. The draft pleadings are then sent to the solicitor who has it typed in a formal manner. The draft pleadings become the plenary summons when it is stamped and filed in the Central Office and the solicitor shows the defence the stamped original and leaves them a copy.

In Liam's proceedings the plenary summons was issued on 6 August 1981. According to Pat McCartan this allowed the State a period of time in which to enter into what is known as an appearance to the plenary summons, and they did that on 13 August 1981. The next step is to file a statement of claim and this sets out accurately upon what grounds the claim is being made.

After the statement of claim is served, it is for the State to file its defence. "What they can and usually do in a case of this complexity," explains McCartan, "is that before they file their defence they raise detailed questions to clarify the statement of claim." McCartan explains that the State raised thirteen specific queries "for which we were obliged to supply them with replies."

These queries were contained in a letter dated 3 October 1981 from the Chief State Solicitor. Liam was able to answer most of these simply with a yes or no. From his answers to the questions it is easy to see that, whether he won or lost the case, once he was in court, he would enjoy his best ever public platform for the issues he spent twenty years campaigning for. Some of the questions he treated with the contempt he felt they deserved. To the question, "Does the plaintiff use any methods of mobility other than a wheelchair?" Liam answered "I use no other means other than my wheelchair except for long distances—in which case I use a car or an aeroplane." To the question "How could his mobility be improved," part of his answer was, "My mobility without a wheelchair can be improved or assisted to precisely the same extent as the mobility of a sack of flour can be improved by carrying it."

Here again Mary Robinson remarks on Liam's confidence regarding the law. Although he was very serious and anxious about the case, he still retained a sense of humour. "He had answered a number of questions and then he puts down, 'Over to you three legal geniuses.' "

"This is where our first stumbling block arose," says Pat McCartan. He says in order to get the answers to queries raised by the State, he had to ask court staff direct questions. "We didn't want to pretend we did not know the answers in our replies because if we did we would be showing a sign of weakness." The aim was to "put the State on unsure ground by showing a higher degree of knowledge of the facts and statistics they were looking for." Pat McCartan says they needed to find out about the running of the court, how lists are drawn up, how people are notified, what Liam's chances were of being called again in a lifetime. If it was found that their knowledge of the mechanism for jury selection was very low, then the defence would simply deny everything.

At this stage it is important to point out that while Liam's case was being processed, in the High Court in 1981 and in the Supreme Court in 1983, Mrs Nora Draper, a disabled woman, brought an action claiming that because she could not travel to the polling booth and there was no provision for her to cast her vote by post, she was denied her constitutional right as a member of the electorate.

There are obvious parallels between the Draper case and the one Liam had pending. However it must be pointed out there is one important difference; Mrs Draper was not looking for access to the polling station. It was stated that since 1980 she had been confined to her house and could not be taken to a polling station by any means without causing her severe physical discomfort and a risk to her health, which she had been medically advised to avoid. If you are medically unfit to travel to a polling station, you will be medically unfit to travel to a court to do jury duty. Liam himself was emphatic on the distinction between being disabled and being sick. It is relevant that in dismissing the Draper appeal in the Supreme Court, Chief Justice O'Higgins declared, "The State may well regard the cost and risk involved in providing special facilities for particular groups as not justified having regard to the numbers involved."

So what would have happened had Liam got to court? Senator Robinson says they would have relied more on the law than on the constitutional point as in the Draper Case. She says emphatically, "they had no power to remove his name like that just because they thought it might be irritating or frustrating for him."

When asked why he thought Liam would not have been successful had his case reached the courts, Pat McCartan, like Mary Robinson, gives the statements in the De Burca case as not having established the right of people to sit as jurors.

"But does that mean he was wasting his time and energy?"

"Oh no,"McCartan insists. "Even if we had gone into court ultimately for a hearing and we got a ruling against us in the High Court, we were then going to the Supreme Court and then to the European Court of Human Rights and all along the way we were going to have a trail of publicity and quite often with actions like this, while you might not get a favourable judgment it creates publicity and it embarrasses the courts." He reiterates their intention of ultimately having recourse to the European Courts, "where if we had gone on the basis that the whole of Ireland couldn't supply one courtroom in which a paraplegic or person confined to a wheelchair could be admitted for the purpose of giving duty as a juror it would make us look like an ass. So irrespective of the law we were going to see this one through because we had Ercus Stewart's opinion from June 1981 that it was a good issue and worth pursuing."

Senator Robinson agrees. "In some ways sometimes you can make progress by taking a case even if you don't win. But also," she cautions, "sometimes in these areas if you don't win, then you take two steps backwards."

There can be no doubt that with his mind, Liam Maguire would have seen all the subtleties involved. He would have wanted the case pressed ahead, as expressed above by Pat McCartan. However, the replies to the State's notices for particulars were never drafted.

There were three happenings during 1982 and 1983 that perhaps understandably struck a blow at everybody's enthusiasm. Primarily there was the judgment in the Draper case that the State was entitled to have regard to the costs when considering facilities for minority groups. Secondly, as a consequence of a fire in the High Court, court No 4 was made partially accessible. Finally, at around this time case the onset of the illness which was to lead to Liam's death.

For the purposes of research the author went to inspect the Four Courts. While there are concessions towards accessibility in the form of a ramp from the car park off Mortimer Place, they are obviously intended to facilitate the victims of accidents involved in compensatory claims, and not for disabled people taking an active part in the judicial system. The toilet the author was shown as being for disabled people, and to be opened with a special key, is totally unsuitable for the vast majority of paraplegics. No, Liam Maguire would certainly not have been satisfied with this, and would see the need for his claim to take its course as being as great as ever.

Nevertheless, one must sympathise with the

three lawyers whose commitment was not in doubt. As Senator Robinson says "In a constitutional case what really happens is that you are weighing carefully, particularly at the stage of finalising the Pleadings. Sometimes you want to get on very quickly because the matter is of great urgency. In this case it was more a matter of weighing the tactics of bringing it forward, considering the position." In the light of Liam's subsequent death, she says she regrets not bringing it forward more quickly.

It is worth pointing out that although the Draper claim was unsuccessful, Mrs Draper was awarded her costs and postal votes for disabled people and others were introduced in Ireland in 1985.

Chapter 14

It seems very obvious that following the long and bitter 1978 strike, Aer Lingus management had decided to get Liam Maguire out of their hair by removing him altogether from their immediate industrial relations scene. This is not unusual, and it is commonly expected by workers that management will get rid of an effective shop-steward by giving him or her promotion. However, most of the managers saw Liam's aggressiveness as "a chip on the shoulder" at being confined to a wheelchair, and according to one source none of them wanted anything to do with him. The exception was Martin Dully, Aer Lingus's sales manager at the time.

Dully had known Maguire since Liam first joined the airline before his accident. He talks about the 1960s as the most exciting decade in recent history, and Maguire coming into an emerging industry. "Aviation was begining to take off in a big way in Ireland, and working for Aer Lingus was a prime job." As we know, Liam's ambition was to be a pilot, but because of a slight medical problem, which was expected to sort itself out within a year, he joined traffic control temporarily. Dully remembers Liam as smart and intelligent; a quick thinker with a promising career until tragedy struck.

Dully says although his Aer Lingus friends kept in touch it is understandable that there was "a great loneliness about that kind of accident and the long recovery involved in it." He says; "There was a bitterness there in Liam which gradually mellowed." While his young Aer Lingus colleagues were taken up with the era of The Beatles and the Irish showband scene, Martin Dully considers that Liam had time to think "and as a result he formed values then which he subsequently took back into this business with him." Dully believes that before his accident Liam was shaping out to be a capitalist, but afterwards, "in thinking about his condition he began to see his life as it ought to be."

Martin Dully offers the following interpretation of Liam's ideas: that instead of business being about profit all the time it ought to be about the welfare of the employees. "His dedicated socialism, being to the fore of any delegation whether the issue was workers' pay and conditions or accessibility for the disabled, and his intolerance of the opposing viewpoint, were not attributes to endear him to management." Dully says that Liam thought that a state company such as Aer Lingus should concern itself with the community as a whole—which includes the elderly and the handicapped—because its shareholders are the community.

When Liam moved from ground operations to Aer Lingus sales he became a specialist in services for disabled passengers. As far as we can make out, he was given virtually a free hand. Martin Dully writes; "Liam's work style was individualistic and at times unconventional. Quite often he wrote a hand-written letter to me seeking approval for an overseas journey or for some new contact to be established. My own technique was often to write 'go ahead' on his letter and send the lot back to him as his authority." Liam's files concern the possibilities of developing for Aer Lingus a holiday market in disabled travellers. In his paid capacity with Aer Lingus he was now concerned with accessibiltiy to hotels and holiday resorts in Ireland. Thus he was meeting such people as the Minister of Tourism (11 August 1980) and Bord Failte on these matters. Bob Bowman of Bord Failte spoke to us about discussing with Liam the potential of tours in Ireland on accessible coaches and said there is a commercial company in Britain operating such tours. Bowman also said Bord Failte produced a guide to accessible accommodation in 1981, which was revised in 1985.

The move to Aer Lingus sales in effect made Liam a full-time activist in the international movement of disabled people. In 1980 he attended ten or twelve conferences in different countries, often flying from one to the other before returning to Dublin. Kathleen S Miller writes of meeting Liam during May in Washington DC where he gave a presentation on trade unions and disabled people in Ireland. Ms Miller writes: "Some called him angry and abrasive—somehow I saw something more than that but wasn't certain what it was until much later." London-based Derek Lancaster-Gaye writes of travelling with Liam on a number of occasions to Luxembourg or Bonn, since they were members of the same Action Européenne Des Handicappés committee. In October 1980 there was controversy over the International Air Transport Association requiring a medical certificate from disabled passengers. Liam was very much involved in the Access to the Skies programme and its director, Ellis Reida, was just one of several disabled activists Liam was in constant contact with in America.

For Liam the United States was something of a mecca as far as the movement of disabled people in their demand for civil rights was concerned. In our 1981 interview he spoke to the author about the development during the 1960s and '70s of the American Coalition of Citizens with Disabilities. He talked about the "apartheid" between war veterans and other disabled people. He said there was an entirely separate hospital and rehabilitation system for the veterans who felt themselves in an elitist position relative to disabled people generally. "However," Maguire said with appropriate cynicism, "sense began to prevail among the veterans when they saw, after arriving home to the citations and rubber medals, that they were in the same position as other disabled people. People didn't want to know about veterans in terms of housing, employment and transportation." Maguire explained that some of the "vets" began to realise that unless all disabled people joined forces, they would be wasting their resources.

Eunice Fiorito, the first president of ACCD, says the organisation evolved as a result of President Nixon vetoing the Rehabilitation Act of 1972. A loose group of people then held a demonstration in the Senate, but failed to have the veto overturned. A year later a second Rehabilitation Act was was passed after a more organised campaign by disabled people. It was the success of 1973 that pointed the way towards a national coalition of all disabled people. The ACCD became an umbrella body for organisations in different states.

Liam became acquainted with people such as Judy Heumann, Ed Roberts and Eunice Fioritio, all of whom see the cause of disabled people very much in political terms, in the context of the overall civil rights movement.

Judy Heumann first met Maguire at the 1972 world congress of Rehabilitation International in Sydney, Australia. A polio victim, Heumann talks of growing up in New York without any positive role models of disabled adult women to give her and her family encouragement for her future. When she was five, her mother attempted to enroll her in the local school and was told by the principal that she would be a fire hazard. Heumann's parents got her private tuition and involved her in after school-hours activities. Yet Judy missed not being with the other children during school hours and says that her social skills were not developing. When she started going to special school with other disabled children, she says that she could talk about her feelings as a disabled person for the first time, although she did not learn very much because the teachers thought their students had no future in society.

Heumann's mother became an active campaigner when a child they knew was refused entry to high school. Her mother was prominent in forming "Parents Together" which started meeting the education authorities and transport authorities about getting the children to school. Heumann says this was her first experience "of how to begin to makes changes occur." Parents Together sought support from the conventional organisations providing for the needs of children with disabilities, but "The March of Dimes" said they did not want to get political; they just wanted to raise money and provide services.

Heumann says things did begin to change and disabled children were going to non-disabled high schools. She talks of the early 1960s when John F

Kennedy was elected President as a time of hope. "But at that time there really wasn't any disabled movement that I could get involved in for myself to begin to make changes for my own life." She talks about being emotionally struck by Martin Luther King's famous speech "I Have A Dream."

While blacks were complaining about high unemployment and their children having few role models of black adults to look up to, Heumann says: "As far as I was concerned as a disabled individual, I didn't even know if we grew up." She said she did not read about disabled people in books or see them on television except for a negative and sometimes frightening image in films such as *The Hunchback of Notre Dame*, and Captain Hook in *Peter Pan*. The only other image Judy Heumann had was of charities that encouraged people's pity for disabled children, and gratitude at not having a disabled child, in order to raise money. "That was a very horrible experience, to realise that people were giving money so that they wouldn't be somebody like me."

These experiences that Judy Heumann describes are universal to disabled people everywhere, but more than anywhere else, for whatever reason, the American disabled community decided they had had enough.

Against the backgound of general political turmoil in the United States in the late 1960s—the assassinations of Robert Kennedy and Martin Luther King, the ongoing campaign for civil rights for blacks and the women's movement—Judy Heumann says that all across the country there were pockets of disabled people organising. They developed a network and people were phoning each other to discuss their concerns and their actions.

Judy Heumann wanted to teach. She passed her exams, but failed to get medical clearance. The doctor even wanted to see her going to the toilet. In Chicago Eunice Fiorita, who became blind at sixteen, had similar experiences. She proved her vocational counsellor wrong by getting her degree in three years, but was refused a teaching post by the state of Illinois; "That then brought to me an awareness of the unfair way people were being discriminated against," says Fiorita.

When Heumann started talking to her disabled friends her personal battle to be allowed to teach became a part of the overall movement of disabled people in New York. Through her story being publicised in the *New York Times*, she found a lawyer to give his services free, and got more and more publicity. After twelve months Heumann won her case, and did teach for three years.

Heumann's lawsuit led to the formation of an organisation named "Disabled In Action" and a State law was passed that anybody qualified to teach could not be discriminated against because of a disability.

However, the real hotbed of the movement by the disabled seems to have been in Berkeley, California. In the early 1960s some disabled students did attend Berkeley University, but they resided in a hospital unit and had no opportunity to participate in student life. Under the leadership of Ed Roberts—paralysed from the neck down since he was fourteen, who was studying political science—the disabled students started to protest. It is important here to note that Roberts has a respirator on his wheelchair to help him breathe. He says he was the first disabled student on the campus and it was clear that he was not welcome there; "they thought

I was going to die or something." His main problem was finding suitable accommodation. He sleeps in an iron lung and the dormitories were too small. He says the authorities were relieved because they thought he would not be able to stay. Then he found that the student health centre had a whole floor vacant and the head doctor allowed him in there. Roberts says he was doing well academically but became dissatisfied with the difficulties of moving around the campus and the "awful attitudes on the part of some of the professors." He admits that his own handicaps are so severe, that once the college had accepted him there were no problems about taking anyone else. Roberts says that after three or four years there were twelve severely disabled students, and when they began to protest they called themselves the "Rollin Quads," "Quads" being short for quadriplegic which is caused by a break higher in the spine and is therefore a more severe disability than paraplegic. Roberts continues: "We really began to feel we were fighting for our own independence, and that there was a future for us out in the community. We really had to think through how to do it; how were we going to make ourselves free." He told this author that while they were achieving an accessible campus they could not move about the city. So when road repairs were being carried out they went to City Hall and said it would be possible to put in curb-cuts at the same time at no extra cost.

Judy Heumann moved from New York to California, and became Deputy-Director of the Centre of Independent Living, under Ed Roberts. In California, Judy Heumann says, it became clear to her that in order to build a strong movement it is necessary to provide services because so many people were living in institutions unnecessarily and it was essential to provide transport for the more severely disabled to come to meetings.

As well as providing services such as wheelchair repairs and home adaptations, CIL runs training courses for disabled people to employ their own home help. In the early days California did have an Independent Care Programme. Ed Roberts says the first thing CIL had to do was to reshape that programme to ensure the money went straight to the disabled person: "So you could hire and fire and pay your own attendant, so you would be in control."

Ed Roberts is very strong on the fact that Independent Living is a political movement rather than just a social service agency. He argues that when you talk about accessibility and individuals having control of their own lives you are talking about fundamental changes in the political system. He says the doctors who do a good job saving disabled people's lives do a better one in preventing the same people reaching their full potential.

Judy Heumann tells the story of how they won accessible public transportation in Berkeley. Over the years the authorities said the buses would not be made accessible because it was too expensive; non-disabled people did not want them and disabled people would not use them. The ultimate step in the campaign came when over 100 disabled and non-disabled people blocked the entrance of the bus station in San Francisco at 4.30 p.m. one week-day. Where they sat also blocked a bridge and no traffic could cross. When the police came they were in two minds between telling the disabled people they were doing a wonderful courageous thing and telling them it was time to go home. The disabled people stayed put and told the non-disabled supporters to move to the side, knowing that the police would be more inclined to arrest the able-bodied. Those who were disabled sat alone in front of the buses. Finally the police had no choice but to arrest them. Judy Heumann says they had great problems lifting them and their wheelchairs into the police vans; that one man weighed about eighteen stone with a wheelchair weighing at least twenty stone. They were arrested, but the charges were dropped. However, Heumann says, the transit authorities finally realised after five or six years that the campaign would not stop. Speaking in 1984, Heumann said as from November of that year, 500 of 800 buses were due to be made accessible.

To meet Ed Roberts for the first time is an inspiration to any severely disabled person. Despite the severity of his handicaps, he seems in full control of his own life. The author met him at a ten-day conference in 1985, and he had a helper constantly near at hand who had to do such things as take money from his wallet. Yet Roberts comes across as a full and dynamic personality with the helper discreetly in the background except when needed. Liam Maguire seemed fond of quoting Roberts saying: "Hopefully this, the rights of disabled people, is going to be the last great civil rights struggle."

In June 1980 Liam attended the world congress of Rehabilitation International, in Canada, a congress that saw disabled people coming together internationally in pursuit of their rights and dignity. Maguire is most evocative in his interpretation of the evolution of Disabled Peoples' International. He said that at the 1972 Rehabilitation International World Congress in Sydney "we had plenty of experts—doctors, sociologists, and so on—telling us what it was like to be in a wheelchair, or to be blind or deaf or whatever, and there were a few token cripples there." After a meeting separate from World Congress the disabled people in Sydney issued a statement that the level of participation by disabled people was unsatisfactory.

In 1976, in Israel, according to Maguire, there was a larger representation by disabled people, but the facilities were "appalling." "We threatened to lie down in front of the buses one night because they had no transportation for us cripples, and suddenly a fleet of taxis came from nowhere." Maguire said that, at the closing of the conference, when invited to introduce a resolution, he took the opportunity to warn Rehabilitation International that there would be many disabled people from North America at the next conference to be held in Winnipeg, Canada, and "unless there is much greater participation by disabled people in matters affecting their own lives you can have your conference inside, and we'll have ours outside." Ron Chandron-Dudley from Singapore remembers that Liam "charged forward and grabbed the mike" and complained very forcefully that the rostrum and everywhere else was most inaccessible. Ellis Reida was also at the 1976 conference and remembers this outburst. Reida writes about Liam: "He was irritated with me at the time as I, while agreeing with the substance of his charge, felt that politically he could accomplish more in a different direction."

Although the Americans seem to be the major influence in DPI, the initiative did not come from there Ron Chandron-Dudley says that in 1980 he was in Sweden, and talks of discussing with Bengt Lindqvist of Sweden a resolution that the majority

of the RI council should be made up of disabled
people. Maguire told the author he thought this ill-
advised because it raised the problem of defining
disability.

Jim Derksen of Canada gives an interesting
perspective on the situation in the host country
approaching the Rehabilitation International
World Congress in 1980. As might be expected,
disabled Canadians seem similar to the Americans
in their assertiveness. They too have gained
significant concessions from their government. Jim
Derksen was the National Co-ordinator for the
Coalition of Provincial Organisations of the Handicapped. He says in many ways COPOH was
becoming politically more credible than the established organisations of professionals working for
the handicapped. They feared the publicity and
government attention given to the RI congress
would reverse this trend: "that in fact it would
strengthen the traditional service providing medically based structures." Derksen says in the two
years previous to the world congress COPOH negotiated with government. As a result of these negotiations COPOH got enough funding to engage
fifty activists who recruited disabled people from all
over the world to come to the congress. There were
also special meeting rooms laid on for disabled
delegates, with translations in Spanish and
French.

Derksen claims that the translation laid on by
Rehabilitation International was poor. He also
talked about COPOH having a big display entitled:
"Equal Partners in Participation," and members
wore badges with the same motto. COPOH also
produced a daily newssheet during the conference
which reviewed the speeches of the previous day

based on a questionnaire filled out by disabled delegates. This newsheet was produced at 2 a.m. and put under the bedroom door of all the delegates; "The first thing everybody read each morning, because it came under their door, was the opinions of disabled people. We gave dinosour awards to those who were most traditional and hidebound in their thinking, and star awards to those who were the most progressive and liberal. It started to be the talk of the whole congress and the thing that was most eagerly looked for was our little paper." This led to an atmosphere of revolt.

Lindqvist's resolution was rejected. Jim Derksen says the way it was defeated, "the paternalistic kind of speeches that were made by the RI authorities," fuelled the fires of discontent. "They were so false," Bengt Lindqvist says with feeling, "because on the one hand they said 'Oh yes, we think you should speak for yourselves,' and on the other hand they were not willing to change anything." The disabled people, as in Sydney, held their own meeting. Maguire said there were about four hundred disabled people and they met on two successive days; from 6 p.m. till 10 p.m. and from 6 p.m. till twelve midnight.

Jim Derksen says; "Liam was someone who made a big impression on us all because he spoke like a proud man, he spoke like a very assertive man, he became angry, and he wasn't afraid to express himself—he spoke as someone who had ties with the labour movement; he used the terminology of labour, 'solidarity,' and 'brotherhood of man.' " Gini Laurie, editor of the *Rehabilitation Gazette* in Missouri, recalls Liam's holding a large room of disorganised people from all over the world with a combination of charm and strength. She says he created a magic and excitement that only comes from real leaders such as Kennedy, Roosevelt, and Winston Churchill. While the initiative came from the Swedish delegation and the Canadians set the atmosphere, most people we spoke to seem to think Liam's oratory was the force that made the determination crystallize.

The disabled people at the Winnipeg conference decided to form a consumer organisation, and this became Disabled Peoples' International. A steering committee, with two representatives from five different regions, was elected. Maguire became one of the European representatives, and Bengt Lindqvist of the organisation for the blind in Sweden the other.

Liam would have had much in common with Bengt Lindqvist and Ron Chandron-Dudley. Ron Chandron-Dudley says he was reasonably successful in getting Singapore trade unions involved in the rehabilitation of workers who were injured in industry. Bengt Lindqvist says: "I had found another socialist who could put together the situation of disabled people and the general policies in our societies. From then on," Lindqvist says with enthusiasm, "we were friends."

Bengt Lindqvist talked to us about the history of disabled people in Sweden, going back to the 1880s when organisations of blind and deaf people first began. In 1942 a confederation representing different disabilities, named HCK, was formed. HCK has grown over the years, and now represents twenty-five national organisations with 340,000 paying members. HCK is now a legitimate part of Swedish democracy for negotiating with the Government, but Bengt Lindqvist assures us that the old aggressiveness comes back when it is found necessary.

Liam was impressed with HCK. In 1981 he said the disabled in the Nordic countries, as well as in America, are effective because they have laws underwriting their position.

The steering committee, formed in Winnipeg, was to do three things: write a constitution; establish contact with consumer organisations of disabled people; and, thirdly, organize a world congress in 1981. The committee met three times—in San Francisco, Dublin and Toronto. Funding came from various international sources, and for the meeting in Dublin Aer Lingus provided free airfares. Liam took the task of preparing the constitution. He gave the organisation a three-tier structure. The National Assembly would be an organisation or group of organisations of disabled people. The National Assembly sends delegates to a Regional Assembly, which elects a Regional Council. The Regional Councils elect delegates to the World Council which in effect is the executive of Disabled Peoples' International. Every fourth year DPI holds a World Congress open to anybody. The World Congress has a consultative status. DPI's constitution is firmly based on that of the International Labour Organisation which Liam told us with enthusiasm is the only surviving body from the Treaty of Versailles. He calls the ILO a distinguished organisation of employers, trade unions and governments. Maguire claimed that the ILO was the first organisation to recognise the United Nations and the first to be a non-governmental advisory body to the UN.

The Toronto meeting was the steering committee's last, and all was ready for the first World Congress in Singapore.

In Singapore, DPI's constitution was adopted,

and the delegates produced a manifesto and a plan of action. The opening paragraph of "The Singapore Declaration" points out that there are 500 million disabled in the world, and 100 million are severely disabled solely because of malnutrition.

Maguire acquired a passionate interest in the latter statistic. The paper he read at the Singapore congress, entitled "Technology Transfer" points out that while disabled people in the developed countries have a basic right to an accessible environment, he asks: "But what about the basic human right to nourishment?" Like all Liam's work this piece is not just vague generalities; he condemns the spending of one million dollars every hour of every day on the arms race. One of the statistics he illustrates is that the twenty million dollars to produce one modern tank could sustain 24,000 adults for one year. The inner rage of Liam Maguire was not self-pity; it was a passionate feeling for his fellow man.

Chapter 15

Harry Ellis says the Parkes Hotel campaign is an instance of Liam wanting something too quickly, and demanding the impossible. This is not a criticism of Maguire on Ellis's part, more the despairing cry of one friend for the other whom he sees taking on seemingly impossible tasks. In the same tone Ellis tells us how he often told his friend, "You'll never get a flat world, Liam."

If his battle to be considered eligible for jury duty shows that nothing was too big for Maguire to take on, the Parkes Hotel affair shows he didn't neglect little things. Compared to the other things he was involved in at this stage, Parkes Hotel was relatively small fry. It was a small drama confined to the stage of Dun Laoghaire District Court. Yet it must be seen as comparable to a tiny ball-bearing in the timing mechanism of a jumbo-jet engine. If it works out right then the whole thing could take off.

The Parkes Hotel campaign shows the same patient step-by-step build-up, like moves on a chessboard, as the jury case. It began on 14 September 1980 when the press reported that the South County Hotel (as Parkes was then) in Stillorgan, Co Dublin had been purchased by Mr Louis Murray and others. That evening Liam delivered a letter to Murray saying that he had been a regular cutomer of the hotel for the past two years and pointing out the lack of wheelchair-accessibility on the premises. He enclosed the National Rehabilitation Board's Minimum Design Criteria and offered every possible assistance. There was no reply. On 4 April 1981 Liam wrote to Louis Murray:

> Undoubtedly you are an extremely busy person and that is why I received no acknowledgement or acceptance of my offer to be 'available to discuss this matter at any mutually convenient time.' As you are currently in the process of reconstruction, I earnestly hope that you are providing accessibility. My offer of assistance still stands.

The next letter in the Parkes Hotel file, to Liam from Nuala Fennell TD, is dated 21 August 1981 It refers to a telephone conversation the previous week and goes on to say: "I wrote to Mr. Louis Murray, expressing my surprise at the glaring omission in his renovations, and suggesting that it could not be too late to adapt to suit everyone instead of some. I'll be in touch when I get an answer."

On 25 August 1981 Louis Murray wrote to Nuala Fennell to say that not providing a ramp for the disabled was an oversight. He expressed regret and said he would instruct his architect to put a ramp at each entrance as soon as possible.

On 11 September Liam wrote to Nuala Fennell noting the "vagueness" of Louis Murray's commitment to provide ramps "as soon as possible." Maguire continues: "There is also a complete lack of reference to wheelchair-accessible toilet facilities. Frankly, I am somewhat less than enthused about the stated regret for his oversight—an oversight which any objective assessment of the evidence available would almost certainly deem to be deliberate."

In the meantime Liam Maguire had been in touch with solicitor Pat McCartan, who at the same time was working with him on the jury case. Liam conveyed the following to Naula Fennell: "Having taken advice on this matter I am in the process of lodging an objection to the renewal of his [Louis Murray's] licence at the Annual Licencing Date, 24 September, in the Dublin Metropolitan Court. The grounds are currently being written up by me in consultation with others for one week beforehand. As you have had more success than I in getting a response from Mr Murray," Liam writes to Ms Fennell, "you may wish to communicate this information to him. Should you receive, in writing, a definite commitment that the minimum criteria for access, as published by the National Rehabilitation Board, will be met on a certain date in the very near future, I shall not lodge the objection. If I have not heard from you by Wednesday (16th) [September] next I shall assume Mr Murray is indifferent to this matter."

The three-page objection lodged in the courts on 16 September, in the name of Harry Ellis, as well as Liam Maguire, is an impressive document. Typical of Maguire's style, it cites the Treaty of Rome, the United Nations General Assembly, and the Irish government's Draft Building Regulations, on the right of access for disabled people.

The case was heard on 24 September. Newspaper reports mention Harry Ellis as taking the case on behalf of Liam Maguire and himself. It appears that Maguire was not there. Possibly he was abroad attending a DPI or Access to the Skies conference, or on Aer Lingus business. Having a court case pending was no reason to keep him at home worrying unnecessarily. On the other hand, he might have been in hospital, as this was about the time of the beginning of the illness that eventually led to his death. In court, solicitors for Louis Muuray said: "We do intend to facilitate disabled people at some point, but we cannot do it until the road works outside the hotel are completed." Justice Brendan Wallace said he would like to see the problem resolved by consultation between the two parties involved and adjourned the case until 18 November.

On 22 October, the *Irish Independent* carried a report on the formal re-opening of Parkes Hotel and the "new sophisticated Flamingo Nightclub." The report, including a photograph of Louis Murray with four pretty girls holding cocktails, is very chic. In stark contrast none of the media seems to have shown any interest in Liam's press release on 17 November outlining the case so far.

There followed several adjournments to allow discussion between all those concerned. Liam was becoming ill at this time. Harry Ellis remembers bringing architects and barristers into the hospital. According to Ellis Liam's continuing interest in the case was one of the things which kept his spirits up. The letter to Pat McCartan dated 1 March 1982 from barrister Tom O'Connell, who was now acting for Ellis and Maguire, sums up the situation. O'Connell states:

On my last appearance in this matter Mr Ellis was present in court, but not Mr Maguire who is hospitalised. I was informed by solicitors for Parkes Hotel that they were not prepared to accede to the full requirements of our clients because of cost etc. However, they were prepared to make certain alterations i.e. ramping of entrance and access points between different parts of the interior and to provide suitable lavatory facilities with access to it by lift. They were not prepared to make any further concessions other than these, and they were determined to go ahead with the case on that basis. The matter was adjourned by D. J. Magee to the 24th of March 1982.

Mr O'Connell goes on to say that a meeting was held at Liam's bedside that involved himself, Harry Ellis and Liam with Louis Murray's solicitor and architect. Parkes stuck to their guns, and Maguire had to withdraw because to lodge a second objection on the basis that Louis Murray was an unfit person to manage the premises required twelve months' notice. Tom O'Connell writes that to argue that Murray was not a fit and proper person to manage the premises on the basis chosen by Liam "was a strained argument and very unlikely to succeed." To press ahead might have destroyed the existing goodwill of Parkes 'management.

The Parkes Hotel episode is worthy of a chapter if only for Liam's court statement delivered at Dun Laoghaire District Court on 24 March 1982, which needs no editing from the author:

I was unable to attend the last hearing as I have been in hospital since 10th January. The reason that I mention this is that I emphasise that my non-attendance was not due, in any way, to a lack of interest in this matter which we initiated, and which we regard as being of great importance. It is by special arrangement with the National Medical Rehabilitation Centre that I am enabled to attend here today, as I wish to place on the record of this Court some highly relevant statements about disabled people and the law as it stands.

Individual members of the judiciary have on frequent occasions expressed their concern and compassion for disabled people and have courageously done so speaking from the bench. This has occurred at all levels—District Circuit and High Court—in all parts of the country.

It is almost fifteen years since I spoke on 6th July 1967 from this very place in this court before the late lamented Justice Herman Good. On that occasion I was being prosecuted for non-payment of road tax in a case which received wide publicity in Ireland and the United Kingdom.

The reason for my refusal to pay road tax on that occasion was the utter failure of the Government despite repeated representations to recognise the essential nature of a disabled person's car, and, thus, to exempt it from taxes. On that occasion Justice Good said—and his words are emblazoned on my memory forever—"I agree with what you are trying to achieve, and I hope you will be successful. However I must apply the law as I find it, therefore I am obliged to fine you three times your annual tax which amounts to £48/15s—mitigated to £1, one month to pay. Is that all right?"

I must apply the law as I find it.

The law was changed following this case in the Finance Act 1968 so that disabled drivers became exempt from road tax.

In early 1981 Justice Gannon was hearing an injuries compensation case in the High Court. The plaintiff was in a wheelchair and Justice Gannon enquired as to how the plaintiff got into the Court building. On being told about the manhandling and lifting, the Justice made scathing remarks about the lack of facilities for disabled people and suggested that it was time that someone got on with the job of providing them. Regrettably, to date the law has made no such provision.

Many more examples have been brought to my attention of situations where the judiciary have expressed their knowledge of and concern for the situation of disabled people. This is in stark contrast to the law which they are required to apply—a law which has scant regard for the plight of our disabled citizens. To cherish all the children of the nation equally is a pious aspiration of the signatories of the Proclamation of Independence (*sic*). It is not reflected in our Constitution or in our laws. Our Constitution upholds the rights of private property over the rights of the people and our laws disenfranchise disabled people who cannot get to or into a polling booth. Our judiciary are not to blame for these inequities. The blame lies squarely in the laps of our legislators, the members of the Dail, and Seanad Eireann for whom few, if any disabled people can vote. Despite many fine speeches and declarations of intent, these representatives have utterly failed to statutorily provide adequately for socio-economic improvement in the lives of our disabled people. The enormity of this failure is incomprehensible—one tenth of our population is placed in a position of beggary and supplication.

We have no rights.

Ireland is an enthusiastic and respected member country of the United Nations. We have had a high profile on many occasions in the General Assembly and in the Security Council. Our vote, seemingly, is valued and has been lobbied. Our role in international peace-keeping is well known. What is our UN record as regards our own disabled people?

The UN General Assembly adopted on 9th December 1979 Resolution 3447 "Declaration on the Rights of Disabled Persons." Article 9 of the Resolution states, in part *"Disabled persons have the right to live with their families or with foster parents and to participate in all social, creative or recreational activities."*

The General Assembly adopted on 17th December 1979 Resolution 34/154 International Year of Disabled Persons which recognised that *"The International Year of Disabled Persons should promote the realisation of the right of Disabled Persons to participate fully in the social life and development of the societies in which they live and their enjoyment of living conditions equal to those of other citizens."*

The General Assembly adopted on January 30th 1980 a "Plan of Action for the International Year of Disabled Persons." In "Activities at the National Level" Article Q states *"To have regard for the need to introduce legislation to ensure that new building and buildings to which major adaptation are being made are fully accessible to disabled people and to recognise formally that disabled people have the same right of access to all public and social facilities as other people."*

Ireland voted in favour of all these resolutions at the UN in New York. What has been done at home?

Nothing.

Where is the Green Paper on the Rights of Disabled Persons which was promised "before the end of 1981" the International Year of Disabled Persons? The Government has at hand all the information required to enact legislation, The National Economic and Social Council has issued its report, No.50, "Services for Physically and Mentally Handicapped Persons." This Report carries recommendations which could, and should be the basis for legislation on the rights of disabled persons.

William Shakespeare put into the mouth of Shylock the plaintive and angry words of a man representing a second-class people in his time. "I am a Jew. Hath not a Jew got eyes? Hath not a Jew hands, organs, dimensions, senses, affections, passions, fed with the same food, hurt with the same weapons, subject to the same diseases, healed by the same means, warmed and cooled by the same winter and summer as a Christian is? If you prick us, do we not bleed? If you tickle us do we not laugh, if you poison us do we not die?"

Four hundred years later these words are cruelly relevant to disabled people in Ireland—second-class citizens in a nominally Christian country. We have the same desires and aspirations as other people. We are subject to the same emotions of despair and frustration as are our non-disabled fellow citizens—but we experience them more frequently, particularly those of us who are mobility-impaired and wheelchair-users. The built environment is a perpetual nightmare for us—high kerbs, revolving doors, and flights of steps are insurmountable barriers. We are effectively locked out of places of public entertainment and assembly. We cannot use public transport or enter, unassisted, most public buildings—including this one. Our employment and educational opportunities are severely restricted. The crowning injustice is that we are prevented from voting in elections, wherein we could demonstrate our disapproval or approval of our public representatives.

When my colleague Harry Ellis and I entered our objections to the removal of the 7-day licence for Parkes

Hotel, our intentions were twofold. Firstly we intended to highlight the continued ignoring of the needs of disabled people in the provision of facilities of public entertainment. Secondly we wished to provide an opportunity for the judiciary to comment and, if possible, to act upon this failure to provide for a significant proportion of the public when applicants sought licences to serve the public. We say "If possible," because we recognise the limitations within which the law can be interpreted. Yet it is only last week that the newspapers reported the comments of the Solicitor Mr Alan Shatter TD following his successful pursuit of a decree of nullity of a marriage on behalf of a client. He is reported as having said that it was another example of Irish Courts applying modern thinking to the interpretation of an area of law which needs updating and that, once again, the courts are legislating where governments have abdicated their responsibility.

Following full discussions with our legal adviser, Mr Tom O'Connell instructed by Mr Pat McCartan, we have decided as follows: We have regard to the likelihood that if we maintain our objection we are likely to forfeit the goodwill of Parkes Hotel management who have undertaken to carry out certain works by ramping and providing a wheelchair accessible toilet. We acknowledge the goodwill and genuine worthy efforts of the management. However, these do not comply fully with the accessibility minimum criteria as laid down by the National Rehabilitation Board, and consequently, we cannot give our wholehearted endorsement or approval.

Having regard to the express provisions of Section 32 of the Intoxicating Liquor Act, 1960, we withdraw our objection with reluctance.

I would like to record my thanks to my colleague Harry Ellis, to our legal advisers, and most of all to you Mr Justice for the patience and consideration extended to us by the court.

One can only speculate as to what Liam Maguire would have made of the outcome of the Parkes Hotel trial. On the face of it, it was a failure. He had failed to have it stated in Court that Part S of the Draft

Building Regulations, which lays down the requirements of accessibility for any building "to which the public have access whether as of right or by permission and whether subject to or free from charge," should be brought into force. He had no legal basis on which to continue. Yet, as we have seen, he had won considerable concessions from Parkes Hotel. This must count as a moral victory in the midst of defeat. A moral victory was placed on the record in a court of law. One feels sure Maguire would use evidence of this moral victory in what for him was an ongoing fight for justice.

Chapter 16

Because their lower limbs are paralysed and lack sensory awareness and they are sitting all the time, paraplegics are susceptible to pressure sores. These sores can become infected if neglected and allowed to develop. It is part of a paraplegic's living routine to check for these sores.

According to Liam's father, Liam fell in the snow and damaged his hip in January 1982. He spent ten weeks in Our Lady of Lourdes Hospital in Dun Laoghaire near his home and then took off, with the wound unhealed, to Singapore and Tokyo. We do know there was a DPI meeting in Tokyo around this time, and he probably went to Singapore for preliminary discussions with Ron Chandron-Dudley. His father says he also spent twenty-three hours on a flight to Frankfurt during this period.

After his return to Dublin, Liam went from Our Lady of Lourdes Hospital to St Vincent's Hospital for a skin graft, but the underlying bone and tissue were so infected the operation was not a success. He spent some time in Saint James's Hospital, and from there was sent to Doctor Steevens' Hospital. The skin graft that had been put on in St Vincent's had to be removed, and Liam had to sit with his weight to one side. The opposite hip then began to break down. Even at this stage Maguire wanted to be up and about, changing the world for disabled people. He would not agree to rest for ten months.

Ellis Rieda from New York writes of Liam coming to Houston, Texas for a meeting of airlines. "He had requested of me ahead of time to have a medical aide for him to help him dress his open sore. She told me that in her opinion it did not look well. Liam remarked that he had been strongly advised by doctors not to travel, but he wanted to come to the meeting."

On returning from his last conference Liam was in a very bad way with infection. He went back to Our Lady of Lourdes Hospital, and was returned to Saint Vincent's with a view to further bone removal. The infection was now all through his body, affecting organs such as the heart, lungs and kidneys. On the evening of 16 September 1983 Maria Cassidy thought Liam too sick to undergo an anaesthetic. He was due for theatre the next day. Maria was at the bedside, but her nurse's skill could not save him. At 10.45 p.m. he died of toxic heart failure.

We spoke to Maria in the confortable bungalow at Ballymun Avenue that she and Liam had bought. They had had the house for some time before he died, but it needed extensive renovations to make it so that a wheelchair could move about easily. Liam did not hurry in having this work done; Harry Ellis says the house was an example of the way Liam was neglectful of his personal needs in favour of working for the disabled community.

The renovations were completed shortly after Liam died and Maria intended living in the house on her own. "But," she said, "Dublin is a small city and everywhere you went there were memories—every pub you'd pass and every theatre. I got to the stage that when I'd go to the theatre I'd be looking over my shoulder at the place where we used to sit, and two years later I was still breaking up." When we spoke to Maria she was planning to take up a nursing post in Saudi Arabia, and later she settled in Scotland.

It must be said here that other paraplegics, even those who were his friends, believe that Liam was wrong not to stay in hospital. They say he might have been in hospital a year or more, but then he could have picked up where he left off. Paddy Lewis agrees with Jack Kerrigan when he says that he didn't think that Liam ever really accepted the fact that he was disabled. "I think he may have looked at the idea of acceptance as something rather negative—as lying under."

Others, such as Paddy Byrne, who worked with disabled people for many years before his death in 1988, concluded that Liam accepted his disability but he was never going to accept the physical and attitudinal barriers that disabled people are expected to face in the outside world.

We can find as many opinions on Liam Maguire as there are people who knew him, ranging from those who say he was "a chipped personality" to Judy Heumann from New York who first met Liam on a dance floor in Sydney, Australia. She describes him as "a wild guy, a great political person, a wonderful dreamer and an incredibly hardworking person, who touched my life very significantly as I know he touched the lives of many people."

Kathleen S Miller of Michican says what some saw as abrasiveness in Liam she came to see as an "intense commitment to eradicating the inequities that disabled people face."

There was a streak of macho independence in Liam. Talking about the long-drawn out meetings during the 1978 Aer Lingus strike, Paul Boushell says Liam should have lain down for the recesses: "but he would have seen that as weakness on his part, that somehow he was a bit weaker than everyone else, and he had to be stronger than everybody in every way. If the negotiation committee decided they were going to climb Carrauntohill, he'd be doing it too. regardless of what that meant." Boushell says Maguire was absolutely adamant that no concessions be made to that fact that he was in a wheelchair, "which I think was very foolish." Paul Boushell is just one person who says that Liam pushed everything to the limit. Nurse Brid Murphy talks with regret of Liam not coming back to the National Medical Rehabilitation Centre for regular checkups in later years.

Whatever mistakes Liam made regarding his personal life do not take away from his contribution to the disabled movement as a whole. Over the past twenty-eight years disabled Irish people have made great strides. We have come from being hidden away in the back room to being generally accepted as part of the community. It is commonplace now to see a person in a wheelchair in a pub or on the dance floor in a disco. Most young people now are comparatively relaxed in the company of a severely disabled person.

While nobody can claim that this is solely due to Liam Maguire there is no denying his contribution has been massive. Micheal Saunders, chief driver instructor in the Irish Wheelchair Association, can testify to the financial struggle it is for many disabled people to own a car. For people who cannot walk, a car is not a luxury; if they are able to drive it is their only means of independent mobility. Those who can just about afford a car at the moment definitely would not have one but for Liam

Maguire's actions in 1967.

Liam's contribution to accessibility was enormous. If we go by Tom Page of the NRB it seems that but for Liam the international access symbol would have no real meaning in Ireland. This is not meant to take any credit from the other people on the committee, but it does seem that Liam's continuous making of a point got people to think differently. It also shows that he learned the art of compromise in accepting a second symbol of lesser accessibility. In the autumn of 1984, a year after Liam's death, the committee did their second survey with Bord Failte and found ten premises which qualified for the full symbol of accessibility and fifty qualified for the second symbol—accessibility to the wheelchair user with assistance of one person.

The incident in Spain with John McCarthy (already described), when Liam insisted on taking down the bathroom door, is interesting. This is the only occasion where Liam was so insistent while on a social visit. Perhaps it was because McCarthy is a trade union activist like Liam and the sort of person who would see the significance of his action. Paul Boushell does say that if his Aer Lingus colleagues booked a room for an occasion and it was upstairs, Liam would let them know what he thought. Usually he said: "Here you are again and you never thought of me or anyone else who might be in a wheelchair." It would be wrong to give the impression that Liam carried on to the point of being unpleasant. The number of people who considered him a warm sensitive character and liked being in his company is a repudiation of that.

The episode in the Department of the Environment when Liam refused to go higher than the fifth floor because he couldn't reach the buttons in the lift is a different situation. There he was in a government building, where decisions are taken, and to him that was the place to make his point. He was, on the other hand, a frequent visitor to Dublin's Peacock Theatre where he had to be carried up and down stairs.

The legacy of goodwill and understanding toward disabled people in the Irish trade union movement is very real. Trade unionists such as Peter Cassells of the Irish Congress of Trade Unions, John Hall of the Association of Managerial and Scientific Staffs, as well as Liam's personal friend John McAdam, certainly see the demands of disabled people as legitimate political issues, in a way their predecessors of thirty years ago would not have done. This is solely due to the work of Liam Maguire. However, this goodwill is only a candle-flame blowing in the winds of normal trade union concerns. If it is to be kept alive the initiative must come from disabled people themselves. Brian Malone of the Irish Wheelchair Association assures us that the link with the trade union movement is being maintained. He says that when the ICTU meet the government on social issues, the submissions of the IWA are on the table with everything else.

Again and again throughout our 1981 interview, Liam emphasised that the first most vital change, "from a recipient mentality to a participative one," has to be within disabled people themselves. "They must see things such as accessibility and employment, and adequate social welfare which would enable them to live independently if they could not get suitable work, as entitlements." He seemed to have had a deep conviction that disabled people in Ireland are too grateful for concessions made to them by government.

Irish disabled people—it seems a part of the Irish character generally—have little appreciation of the power of group action. Some years ago at the AGM of the Irish Wheelchair Association a man too disabled to drive a car proposed that people in his position should be given concessions in the same way as disabled drivers. The suggestion was opposed on the grounds that the government might take back what was already given if it was pushed too hard. It is too easy to condemn the opposer of the motion as selfish, but there seems little appreciation that concessions such as tax relief on petrol were won—mainly by Liam Maguire—aggressively, with the courage of conviction. Contrast this with Judy Heumann's lawsuit in New York leading to the formation of the organisation named Disabled In Action. Maria Cassidy talks about Liam fighting about accessible public transport with the NRB board, which, it seems, actually supported CIE on the issue. She says at that stage he felt very much alone, and even disabled people themselves seemed unwilling to be angry.

In the late 1970s a Disabled Action Group did form itself in Dublin, and succeeded in getting media attention for a number of demonstrations. However, it seems that the leaders did not have the maturity to realise that bringing about political change really necessitates slow grind. In America disabled people took to the streets, but it was in conjunction with intense and sustained lobbying of politicians behind the scenes. When one looks at the life of Liam Maguire, it is with the realisation that it was a patient determination that brought him success more than anything else.

The message coming from Liam Maguire, and

people like Ed Roberts in America, seems to be that unless disabled people demand everything—and have the courage to demand it forcefully and aggressively over an interminable period of time—they will be given only the bare minimum. It is worth quoting New York lawyer Curtis Brewer a second time when he says: "The question is, what do we really want in terms of being disabled? Do we want our rights vigorously, or passively expect to have them given to us? If it is the latter, then we are guilty of masochistically compounding the patronization we experience."

As in any sphere of activity, meeting disabled people from other countries has great benefits. It does not mean you are going to adopt everything they say and do, and implant it without alteration into a different economic or cultural setting. Talking to those who are more advanced gives hope and renewed determination; talking to those who are at a similar stage as your own country, but with some differences, is a stimulating experience. This is evidenced by events leading to the founding of the Irish Wheelchair Association. Speaking of the paraplegic Olympics which took place just before the establishment of the association Oliver Murphy says: "We spoke to an awful lot of people at that games about how things were going in their countries, particularly Dutch and Americans. We formed the opinion that this was the time that at home in Ireland something should be started specifically to help people in wheelchairs."

When asked why the IWA did not send any representative to the Second World Congress of Disabled Peoples' International in 1985, Brian Malone, then IWA chairman, said the Association's function was to pursue the cause of wheelchair users in Ireland. He said that Liam could get on an aeroplane at no expense because it was part of his job with Aer Lingus. He argued that the Association could not justify making the required expenditure from scarce resources. While one has to accept the validity of Malone's point, that nobody could travel at the rate Liam could, one feels if we don't maintain some real contact with the disabled international community, disabled people in Ireland will lose out in the long term. DPI seems to offer the best mechanism for doing this.

It is true to say that DPI have so far failed to make the impact an enthusiastic supporter might wish for, but in a letter to this writer, dated 15 June 1987, the head of the secretariat, Mr Jan Johnson, reports steady progress. Johnson writes that DPI now has formal member organisations in seventy countries. He also says they have achieved consultative status with bodies such as the UN, the International Labour Organisation and UNESCO. DPI are also seeking consultative status with the World Health Organisation.

This writer attended the Second World Congress of DPI. There was talk of DPI becoming active, like Amnesty International, on anti-war and human rights issues. As if to prove that not all doctors think disabled people should be seen and not heard, Dr Bengt Lander of Sweden purchased one of the largest yachts in the world and it was to be adapted for use by disabled people only. This peace ship was going to circumnavigate the world during 1986, the International Year of Peace. The intention for the peace ship, in accordance with DPI's Hiroshima Peace Statement of 1982, was that it should visit trouble spots with the message that war causes disability and death. It was very exciting and it seemed it would get DPI the worldwide recognition it needed.

Unfortunately it proved impossible to finance the project. Bengt Lindqvist tells us that the Swedish government was prepared to provide one million kroner, the remaining six to seven million could not be raised, and Dr Lander had to sell the hull of the boat. Jan Johnson writes there is a new committee within DPI which will investigate further what can be done.

At that World Congress Eunice Fiorita told us she saw in Liam a man impassioned for the disabled of the third world. There is ample evidence that Liam had a genuine interest in this area. His files contain data on the sort of wheelchairs there are in underdeveloped countries, and at DPI's first World Congress Liam spoke passionately on hunger.

Not everybody on the international scene always saw eye to eye with Liam. Henry Enns from Canada said Liam believed that the governing body of an organisation should keep tight control. Enns says he had very strong differences with Maguire over this because Enns, who was chairperson of DPI's steering committee, says he believes that the mass of disabled people ought to be involved in policy formation of their own organisation. Colm O'Doherty remembers Liam arguing very forcefully with one person—O'Doherty doesn't know the person's name—when DPI met in Dublin. When asked what the argument was about O'Doherty replies: "Liam, and only Liam, was going to solve the world's problems." Many people recognised this viewpoint in Liam. It could be said that he had a paternalistic attitude to the mass of members who made up an organisation. One person commented: "He was like a good carpenter who made a bad overseer because he had to do everything himself."

Speaking in 1985, when the events that occurred in Eastern Europe in 1989 would have been unimaginable, Canadian Jim Derksen says Liam was naive in his politics: "He was unable to view Moscow and the present regime in the Soviet Union in what I would call a realistic light. He had romanticised it." Derksen says his own politics are to the left, but Liam was unable to accept that, while blind people and deaf people in the Soviet Union are treated very well, wheelchair users are much worse off than anywhere in the world.

The disabled movement in the United States, which Liam admired so much, is not talking about outright socialism. When Ed Roberts talks about a fundamental change in the political system one feels he is thinking of more social spending and less expenditure on the military budget. Some disabled Americans are talking about the issues of independence and self-determination being both left and right issues. Americans are writing books and articles that seek to project disability in somewhat positive, rather than wholly negative terms. One writer calls this a "black is beautiful" phase. One biography, published in 1985, is slightly critical of Franklin D Roosevelt for trying to project a non-disabled image of himself while he was President of the USA.

Everything is not perfect in America. Eunice Fiorita talks of the conflict between different strands of opinions within the disabled movement. She complains that the Centres for Independent Living serve only mobility-impaired wheelchair users and motorised quadriplegics. Others claim that the American Coalition of Citizens with Disabilities is only an east coast organisation, and

Fiorito claims that these people are founder members of ACCD who were not re-elected to office.

The American disabled movement is also under intense pressure from ultra-conservative advocates of fiscal rectitude who question the spending of money on an "unproductive sector of society," which is how it sees the handicapped.

Liam gave his answer to this type of argument to the Union of Students in Ireland on 17 January 1981:

> In times of social and economic stress it is a comparatively easy task to reduce the level of aids and services and justify this reduction by a lesser degree of ability. Of course the inevitable outcome of such a policy, when carried through to its extreme, is best exemplified by the bizarre solution to the "problem" of the handicapped which was adopted less than four decades ago by the architects of the Third Reich.

Epilogue

Six and a half years after Liam Maguire's death the question of equal rights for the disabled has all but vanished from the concerns of Irish politicians. The grants for disabled people to make their own homes accessible have suffered because of financial constraints on local government. Likewise funding from the health boards towards disabled people taking driving lessons now depends on the individual health board's ability to pay, and it is the same with all the other services designed for the disabled. Those that have not been abolished have been severely curtailed and certainly have not kept pace with inflation.

Wth regard to the achievement of an accessible environment it is said that the ground gained has been consolidated: the Office of Public Works has stipulated that all buildings under its control must take into account accessibility for the disabled. Nevertheless the Building Regulations—in draft form for more than twenty years—have yet to be given the force of law. New buildings in the private sector are still being constructed without being accessible to disabled people. The prospect of an accessible public transport system seems so remote that it will take somebody with the dynamism of Liam Maguire to create any new hope of getting it back under consideration.

It has been pointed out to the trade union

movement that it has failed particularly in educating its own members in their attitude to disabled workers. It is said that the average shop floor worker would reject any suggestion that a disabled person be employed alongside him. This seems an area where the trade unions can easily make a real contribution. Let's hope they do so.

Colm O'Doherty says that Liam would be urging disabled people to take to the streets by now. However many disabled Irish people, with a cynical apathy, viewed Liam Maguire as some sort of eccentric. Contrast this with the international scene where he was seen by many as a source of inspiration. He was, as Phil O'Meachair says, like a good carpenter who made a bad foreman because he wanted to do everything himself. Maria herself tells us that she often said to him that he should have at least one person working more closely with him who could carry on his work should something happen. Many—including this biographer—who otherwise admired him greatly, feel that he was too reluctant to bring people into his confidence.

The real sadness is that we will probably never see the likes of him again. Rest in Peace, Liam. You gave me my dignity. As a disabled person you taught me to be unashamed of what I am. All I can say is Thank You.